MW01297097

1

LOSE YOUR MIND AND FIND YOUR PURPOSE

**Dedicated to my wife, Sandy,
who has traveled this journey with me
Also thanks to my 2 dear friends,
Bob Mumford and Mark Hanby**

CHAPTERS

INTRODUCTION
1. Stop Looking For What You Already Have
2. Hide and Seek
3. What is True Righteousness?
4. You're Not Who You Think You Are
5. Position Versus Condition
6. Three Types of People
7. Separation of Soul and Spirit
8. Be Still and Know
9. Who is Your Enemy?
10. The Goal of Your Faith
11. Let "I AM" Say "YES" to the "NOW"
12. Off With Their Heads
13. The Philippians Formula
14. The Watcher
15. Finding Your Purpose

INTRODUCTION

The people who heard Jesus teach, even his own disciples, often misunderstood what he was saying. Once when he was in a boat with them he said, "Beware of the leaven of the Pharisees".

Immediately they began to discuss among themselves that someone had forgot to bring the bread. Jesus said that he spoke in parables, not to explain things, but to hide them (Matthew 10:10-13).

Today, we have an additional obstacle to overcome when we read the Bible. It is call "mistranslations". There are around 900 different translations of the Bible in English alone, not counting the thousands in other languages.

Of these 900 translations, no two of them are identical. The original books were written in Hebrew, Greek and Aramaic and then copies were made in Greek and Latin before they became translated into the numerous languages of today.

Most of the time, we are able to revert back to the Greek wording to find a truer meaning of a word or phrase when there are contradictions in the translation. For example: Hebrews Hebrews 11:3 in the KJV reads, *"Through faith we understand that the **worlds** were framed by the word of God"*.

The word "worlds" found in the verse comes from the Greek word "aionas" which means "eons" or "ages". But we find that this word "aionas" is translated into the following words in different Bible translations: *World, universe, worlds, ages, and time.* While all of these were created by God, they all mean something different.

The writer of Hebrews had one specific thing he was saying when he used the word "aionas". There is a big difference between the meaning of time and universe, or ages and worlds. In this particular verse the translation should always have been "ages".

Another example of mistranslation is when Jesus said, *"For whoever wants to save their life will lose it, but whoever loses their life for me and for the gospel will save it. What good is it for someone to gain the whole world, yet forfeit their soul?"* (Mark 8:35-36 NIV).

In these verses Jesus uses the word "life" twice and the word "soul" once. However, all 3 of these words come from the exact same Greek word, "psuche" or "psyche, meaning soul.

If this were translated correctly it would read, *"For whosoever wants to save his psyche will lose it, but whosoever loses their psyche for me and for the gospel will save it. What good is it for someone to gain the whole world, yet forfeit their psyche?*

It is pretty much agreed that the psyche is the mind. We get the word "psychology" from this word: the study of the "psyche" or mind. So the title of this book comes from the more accurate translation of this verse. "Lose your mind, and find your purpose".

"The mind governed by the flesh is hostile to God; it does not submit to God's law, nor can it do so" (Romans 8:7 NIV). *"And be not conformed to this world: but be ye transformed by the renewing of your mind, that ye may prove what is that good, and acceptable, and perfect, will of God"* (Romans 12:2 KJV).

The verses above are clear about 2 things. Our human thinking mind cannot submit nor obey God's law. Therefore, we need a new mind - - the mind of Christ.

When we are "born again", our human spirit is revived. Our spirit is reawakened, but our soul needs to be restored and our mind needs to be renewed. New believers are saved, but they are carnal - - babes in Christ. They do not yet have the mind of Christ. Remember, God's ways and thoughts are not ours.

It is for this reason that Jesus told us that if we want to find our mind, (psyche), we must first lose it! This book explains the process of losing your mind (psyche) in order to find your purpose.

7

Chapter 1
STOP LOOKING FOR WHAT YOU ALREADY HAVE

The legendary band, U2, sung a song that says, "*I have climbed the highest mountains, I have run through fields, I have run, I have crawled, I have scaled the city walls. But I still haven't found what I'm looking for*".

I can no longer sing that song with integrity, for I am no longer a seeker. I was for many years - - - but not anymore. All my life I had sought for a deeper relationship with God and His Kingdom. I read books, listened to teachers, attended conferences, prayed, fasted, and even had cuff links (can't believe I wore those!) that said "The Kingdom or Bust".

But I am no longer a seeker - - because I *have* found what I was looking for. The search was never meant to be eternal. Jesus made you a promise when he said, "*Seek and you will find*". If you see yourself in the lyrics of the U2 song - - then this book is for you.

There are people who are proud to say that they are seekers. You would think, by their declaration, that seeking was an end in itself. However, Jesus did not say, "Seek, and you will *never* find"! The purpose of seeking anything *is* to find it. So if you are a seeker, this book is for you.

This book is also for those who have found. It is for those who have discovered that the search - - whether long or short, can produce that for which they sought. They do not need this book to help them find, but it will be a confirmation to their arrival. It is a good thing to seek, but a greater thing to find!

If you are not in one of those categories, a seeker or one who has found, this book will probably bore you, so don't waste time reading it. Perhaps at a later stage of your life it can be revisited.

Seeking and never finding becomes a frustrating experience. If it is impossible to find what you seek, then you have wasted your time seeking. The goal of seeking is to find. But there are two extremely important things to understand before you start the search. #1 *What* am I seeking for, and #2 *Where* do I need to be seeking for it?

There are a multitude of "things" that people are seeking for. Eventually they find that "things" can never satisfy them. Wealth, fame, popularity, and power can never satisfy. Some of the most unhappy, miserable people on the planet are wealthy, powerful, and famous.

Even when you find the things you seek, those things are never enough. *"All I need is a little more"* becomes the eternal mantra. The reason people seek those things is because they think that "those things" will provide them with deep, lasting peace, incredible joy, and a sense of complete wholeness - - but they never will.

So really, what they are seeking for is not the "things", but the fulfillment, the peace, and the joy they believe those things can provide. But "things" will never produce lasting fulfilment, peace, and joy. The car, the boat, the house, etc. will quickly lose its initial appeal and become just another "thing" that we own. Even the best relationships cannot bring permanent peace, joy, and fulfillment.

Once you have learned that "things" can never bring you the fulfillment that you are seeking for, your search begins to go deeper - - below the surface. Many people never get to that deeper level of seeking. They spend their entire lives seeking it through material possessions, power, or fame.

Usually the deeper level of seeking will lead us to books, like this one, or mentors and teachers. So you read books, listen to teaching, and follow mentors, hoping that you will find answers from them. This is a good direction to take, but if you stop with the books, teachers, and mentors you will never arrive.

The books (including this one), mentors, and teachers can help tremendously by pointing the way to the ultimate answer within you. They are like arrows pointing you in the right direction - - but they cannot give you the treasure, because you already have it! They help remove the obstacles that have hidden the treasure from you.

The end goal is for you, individually, to find the treasure of righteousness, peace, and joy that has waited, within you, for you to discover. For we have this treasure in earthen vessels.

And that treasure has a Biblical name. It is called the Kingdom of God. The clearest definition of the Kingdom is found in Romans 14:17 (KJV): *"For the Kingdom of God is - - righteousness, peace, and joy - -"*.

The word "righteousness" can easily stop us in our tracks at this point. There are so many wrong beliefs and concepts about the word "righteousness", that I want to take a minute and help define it and then elaborate in a later chapter. "Righteousness" is not rules, regulations, doctrine, nor dogma.

It is simply an alignment of our soul with our spirit so that they are both in tune with God's purpose for our lives. The word has been so greatly distorted, that I will be using the word "alignment" instead of "righteousness" from this point on.

I want you to discard all your religious presuppositions about the Kingdom of God for a moment and just ask yourself the question, "Do I want ultimate fulfillment in my life? Do I want unspeakable joy and indescribable peace?

Do I want to love myself and others unconditionally? Do I want to know my purpose?" If the answer is "yes", then you want to be seeking the Kingdom; whatever that means! And it is not a complex journey of legalistic "do's" and "don'ts".

Paul wrote in a letter to the people in Colossae and said, *"Since you died with Christ to the elemental spiritual forces of this world, why, as though you still belonged to the world, do you submit to its rules: "Do not handle! Do not taste! Do not touch!"? These rules, which have to do with things that are all destined to perish with use, are based on merely human commands and teachings".* (Colossians 2:20-22 NIV)

Legalism, which is doctrines of "do's" and "don'ts", will never lead you to the treasure. If fact, legalism will prevent you from ever finding it. You will live in a prison of performance that projects surface accomplishment, but leaves you frustrated and empty inside. Jesus said that you polish the outside of the cup, but the inside is filthy.

Grace has already provided the treasure for you. All self-effort will only lead to failure. All you have to do is clearly hear and understand what the spirit says and believe it.

In the spiritual realm, the currency for finding what you seek is simply "believing". It is not performance or adherence to legalistic standards. *"And without faith it is impossible to please God, because anyone who comes to him must believe that he exists and that he rewards those who earnestly seek him."* (Hebrews 11:6 NIV)

The only two things you are told to believe in this verse are: #1 That God exists, and #2 That he rewards sincere seekers.

So, what is the first thing you should be seeking? Jesus, the Master Teacher, gave us a clear directive when he said, *"But seek ye first the Kingdom of God, and his righteousness, and all these 'things' shall be added unto you"* (Matt. 6:33 KJV).

It doesn't say seek peace and joy. It says seek the Kingdom of God and his righteousness, which means: alignment. It is the alignment of soul and spirit with God's purpose that brings peace and joy!

The promise is that if you seek first the Kingdom, (through alignment), you not only receive the treasure of peace, and joy, but in addition: all these 'things' shall be added! What are all these 'things'? They are the things you once sought for that could never provide the peace and joy that can only come through alignment.

11

You can enjoy your car, your house, your relationships, your work, and your vacations so much more because you no longer are looking to them for your fulfillment. You have found that inside yourself. It is the treasure hidden in the earthen vessel.

You must quit seeking for 'all these things' and seek first the Kingdom. So, settle that issue once and for all; you now know what you need to be seeking: Alignment that brings peace and joy. The second issue is extremely important also. You need to know where to seek.

God has a habit of hiding things that are valuable. *"It is the glory of God to conceal a thing: but the honor of kings is to search out a matter"* (Prov. 25:2 KJV). The very fact that we have to seek the Kingdom, indicates that it is hidden. Why would God hide his Kingdom from us?

He hid the Kingdom, so that in the process of seeking it, we would let go of all the outward things that would harm us or that could destroy the peace and joy that he has provided, but hidden from us.

It is the process of seeking that brings us into alignment with His purposes. The alignment, the straight path that leads to life, then leads us to peace that passes understanding and joy unspeakable and full of glory!

He then told us that we would never be able to see or enter the Kingdom until we had a spiritual awakening. Jesus told Nicodemus that a spiritual awakening *("You must be born again")* was needed or he could not even see, much less enter the Kingdom.

There are some who have had a spiritual awakening that still have not seen that there is a treasure to be sought and found. There are some who have "seen" but have not sought and "entered".

The human mind cannot see or enter the Kingdom of God. It is a "veil" of "white noise" that prevents you from seeing or entering. It is a spiritual awakening that allows you to see and enter the

12

Kingdom through alignment, that allows you to receive the peace and joy that you long for.

"No eye has seen, no ear has heard, no mind has conceived what God has prepared for those who love him. But God has revealed it to us by his Spirit. The Spirit searches all things, even the deep things of God" (I Cor. 2:9-10 KJV).

So - - where did God hide this incredible treasure that provides alignment, permanent peace, and indescribable joy? He hid it in the last place most of us would think to look - - within us!

"Once, having been asked by the Pharisees when the Kingdom of God would come, Jesus replied, 'The Kingdom of God does not come with your careful observation, nor will people say, 'here it is' or 'there it is', because the Kingdom of God is within you" (Luke 17:20-21 NIV).

Notice that the Kingdom does not come with observation. There are many people who, like the Pharisees, are looking for an external Kingdom to emerge at some point in time. There are others that claim that it is "here" or "there". Some believe that it can be found in books or sacred places. But Jesus made it very plain: *"The Kingdom of God is within you"*.

Also, notice that *he was speaking to the Pharisees, not to his disciples.* Current popular theology would resist the notion that the Pharisees could have the Kingdom within themselves, but that is exactly what Jesus said. They, as well as you and I, contain within our human spirit the Source of all fulfilment.

Now, it is true that the Pharisees would need to be spiritually awakened before they could see, or enter, what was within them, but it didn't change the fact that the Kingdom was there! And, my friend, the Kingdom of God is also within you! Whether you believe it or not, it is still there. It is residing deep within your spirit.

13

"The spirit of man is the candle of the Lord"(Prov. 20:37 KJV).

There is a *"secret place of the Most High"* that provides unending peace and joy that *"passes understanding"*. Why does it "pass understanding"? Because it cannot be found in the thinking process of the human mind.

The peace and joy of the Kingdom cannot be accessed through thought. In fact your thoughts create the barrier that prevents you from finding what you seek for - - therefore the title of this book - - lose your mind!

"But the natural man receiveth not the things of the Spirit of God: for they are foolishness unto him; neither can he know them, because they are spiritually discerned" (I Cor. 2:14 KJV).

So, in summary, you must know what you are seeking for and why. You are seeking first, the Kingdom of God, through righteousness (alignment) in order to live in a realm of peace and joy that can be released to the world. And finally, you must know where to look for it: Within yourself, because that's where He hid it.

As with Nicodemus, the awakening of the human spirit, leads us to begin the search for a Kingdom hidden within ourselves. A treasure that is hidden in the field of our own "being". For, indeed, we have this treasure in earthen vessels.

It is important to understand that this search is not a search to find "salvation". It is a search that God calls us to make that will reveal why we were born - - why we were saved! For, He has saved us, and called us, with a holy calling - - not according to our works, but to His own grace and purpose.

Notice that He didn't call us to save us. He saved us to call us. And that calling is the tug of destiny that draws us into the search for alignment, peace, joy, fulfillment, and purpose. It our human minds, our thoughts that create the greatest blockade to prevent us from finding the treasure hidden within us.

14

THE HIDDEN
darrell scott

Much doctrine and teaching has hidden Your presence
Religion and dogma, distorting Your essence

You're sought by so many, and found by so few
You're easy to find, if the seekers just knew

They go to a building with singing and prayer
They reach out to touch You and hope You are there

They visit Your presence but fail to abide
They don't understand that You're always inside

They claim that they'll find You, whatever the cost
But they don't understand that You never were lost

Stop searching "out there", it's like chasing the wind
For That which you seek for is hidden within!

Chapter 2
HIDE AND SEEK
darrell scott

Hide and Seek - - a game from Source, beckons us each day
Curiosity, of course, makes us want to play

Looking here and looking there, never satisfied
Oh if we would dare to find, all that waits inside

Masquerading in disguise, 'neath mind's endless chatter
Treasure hidden from our eyes, Spirit clothed in matter

Trying - - giving it our best, grasping at illusion
Tiring of the endless quest, ending in confusion

Many never play the game, some begin - - but cease
Sidetracked by their wealth, or fame, never finding peace

But a few embrace the course, seeking 'til they find
Spirit's treasure through the Source, hidden by the mind

The Source of your being lures you through the illusion of the visible, physical world to a condition of dissatisfaction, ultimately bringing you back to the inner, invisible realm. This "Kingdom" is where the treasures of joy, peace, and wholeness, through alignment, are found.

You may be thinking, "God would never purposely lure me into a condition of dissatisfaction", so let's take a look at that misconception before proceeding. It was God who lured Israel out of Egypt with the Promised Land.

He told them they would find wells they didn't dig, houses they didn't build, and vineyards they didn't plant (Deut. 6:11 KJV), but he conveniently left out the fact that there were giants that they would have to fight and walled cities that they would have to defeat.

16

So, he lured them into the wilderness! In another passage, he lured Israel into the desert to prepare her for the good things he provided: *"Therefore, I am now going to allure her; I will lead her into the desert and speak tenderly to her. There I will give her back her vineyards and will make the Valley of Achor a door of hope"* (Hosea 2:14-15 NIV). The Valley of Achor in this verse means "the valley of trouble".

> *"God has a "Ways and Means Committee" specifically designing problems that are intended to help you grow"*
> Bob Mumford (My lifelong mentor)

If you look at the temptations that Jesus endured you can see that it was the Spirit, not the devil, who led him into the desert to be tempted: *"Then Jesus was led by the Spirit into the desert to be tempted by the devil"* (Matt. 4:1 NIV).

So we are lured into this spiritual quest, not realizing that it will cost us our heads. Not realizing that we will lose our minds. The false illusions of reality, created by our thoughts will be exposed. The end result will be the loss of a "carnal" mind in exchange for the "mind of Christ". But, I can tell you with full confidence that the pain is well worth the reward.

Max Planck, who won the Nobel Peace Prize in physics, said that, after having studied physical matter his whole life, he came to the conclusion that there is no such thing as "matter". It is simply the illusion of energy manifesting itself in different forms.

Invisible energy produces what we call physical matter, but the microscope has revealed to us the illusion of that matter as we observe it dissolving into atoms, protons, neutrons, electrons, quarks, and finally dissolving into invisible vibrations of energy.

So a purist could say that energy is real, while physical matter is not - - it is an illusion of reality. That is a true statement and it is important for us to understand if we are serious about knowing who we are and why we are here.

17

We are called "human beings" for a reason. The "human" part of you is physical matter, but the "being" part of you is energy, or spirit. Well, to be totally honest, it is all energy or spirit! It is spirit clothed in matter.

"Matter is, and has always been, the hiding place for Spirit, forever offering itself to be discovered anew." Richard Rohr (from: Eager to Love)

We are in this physical world, but not of it. However, the illusion is so real, that it takes most of us a lifetime just to break through that illusion. We seek fulfillment in a world of illusions. We are lured into believing that satisfaction comes from those illusions. We create a false, egoic "self" that always wants more, but is never fulfilled.

The universal game of "hide and seek" must be played in order for you to discover who you really are. When you seek the "spirit clothed in matter" you are taking the first step on the journey to true self-discovery. You then begin to press through the illusion of the visible in order to discover the reality of the invisible.

Neither thought, force, pressure, intimidation, nor grasping will ever produce the peace and contentment that all humans crave. You can only experience it through detachment and a "letting go" of all that is external, and an alignment with the purposes of God.

The shell of temporary indulgence needs to be shed. Only through detachment from the external and embracing of the internal will you ever know the freedom of who you really are.

This detachment especially applies to the endless chatter and "white noise" of your thoughts. In the poem above (reread it) it says that the treasure is hidden from our eyes beneath mind's endless chatter.

Peace and joy are not the products your thoughts - - - not even your positive thoughts.

18

They are only experienced through a detachment from thought, which leads to an alignment of soul and spirit with the thoughts and will of God.

Many make the mistake of believing that the renewing of the mind is simply to replace negative thoughts with positive ones. Granted, positive thoughts are better than negative ones, but we need much more than a change of thoughts - - we need a complete detachment from our 'carnal mind' in order to access the 'mind of Christ' within us. Some think that renewing the mind means to memorize scripture, but it goes much deeper than that.

None of our thoughts are God's thoughts. He made that clear in scripture. We must detach from our own thoughts and tap into his. This will become clearer in later chapters.

Joy, peace, and love are not positive thoughts. They are spiritual realities hidden deep within your spirit, waiting for you to break through the veil of your busy thought life, by detachment, quiet, and stillness. Like the depths of a large lake in the midst of a storm - - the surface may be in turmoil, but in the depths there is a stillness and peace that is unaffected by outer activity.

Only when you can observe your thoughts and understand that they are not you, will you ever discover your true self. If you are the observer of the thoughts, then the thoughts cannot possibly be you!

Those who have discovered the treasure within, understand that there are 3 phases to your inner quest. The first part of your journey is the "seeking phase". This is where you are seeking alignment, peace, and joy from things, people, or the wisdom of books, religion, teachers, mentors, etc.

It is in this initial phase that you discover that nothing (no thing) can ever open the treasure to you. This first phase of seeking eventually leads you to frustration and despair.

19

The writer of Hebrews spoke of *"striving to enter into rest"*. The first part of your journey is the striving. It produces nothing but emptiness and frustration.

The writer of Ecclesiastes summed it up like this: *"And I gave my heart to seek and search out by wisdom concerning all things that are done under heaven; this sore travail hath God given to the sons of men to be exercised therewith. I have seen all the works that are done under the sun; and, behold, all is vanity and vexation of spirit."* (Eccl. 1:13-14 KJV)

It is God who prompts the seeking, as an exercise in futility. *"This sore travail hath God given to the sons of men to be exercised therewith"*. That's why in the poem I called it "a game from Source".

Notice that in the above verses the seeking was for "wisdom *concerning all things"* and *"the works that are done under the sun"*. The seeking ended in frustration!

It is your soul that does the searching, prompted by God. It is to teach you that nothing can be found outside of yourself that will satisfy. It is waiting to be found within you.

It is this frustration, which finally brings you to a point of resignation. You realize, as Jesus did, that *"I can of mine own self, do nothing"* (John 5:3). This is the beginning of wisdom. Also, notice that it was the *spirit* that was vexed, not the soul. The spirit is where the treasure lies.

The spirit knows all things, even the deep things of God (I Corinthians 2:10). The spirit is vexed because it realizes the vanity of the soul searching for answers through religion, doctrines, people, or things.

The second part of your journey is the "finding phase". It takes you within.

Instead of reaching, grasping, and controlling, you learn to detach from your thoughts and efforts and to enjoy the treasure found only through awareness in stillness.

It is in this second phase that you experience personal enjoyment and fulfillment. There is a temptation to remain in that place of bliss, enjoying the peace and joy, without having to interact with others in the illusionary world that we have escaped from.

Those who "enter the rest" of sacred stillness know of treasures unspeakable to those whose eyes are blinded by thoughts and things. Thoughts and things can be enjoyed from a state of awareness, but can never produce that state.

Thoughts and things are products of past and future. We cannot live in either of these. Memory thoughts imprison us in the illusionary past. Vision thoughts imprison us in the nonexistent future. Memory is "I was". Vision is "I will be". I AM is always living in the present, in the "now".

The purpose of detaching from thought and entering the stillness within is to amplify the awareness of the present.

There is a divine "teasing" that allows temporary satisfaction, but never permanent fulfillment, until we are abandoned to the "now". Only when "I AM says, 'yes' to the 'now'", will we know who we are and why we're here. I AM is who you really are. It is the spirit within you that is the candle of the Lord. It is the spark of divinity that was awakened and prompted the seeking.

We have learned the duality of "human being". The "being" is *who* we are. The "human" is the *expression* of who we are. We are the "spirit clothed in matter".

When expression poses as Source, frustration is the result. When expression yields to Source, fulfillment is inevitable.

21

The third phase of your journey is "release and wholeness". The peace and joy that you experience is not there just for your benefit. It is there to be released so that all those you come in contact with can eat of its fruit and become hungry for the same reality that you have found.

As they partake of the fruit from your life, seeds are planted in theirs. This is the greatest phase of all, the phase of unconditional love.

We find frustration in the first phase where we are seeking for answers outside ourselves. This is the "righteousness" phase where alignment, through seeking, is taking place.

We find great peace in the second phase where the Kingdom becomes real to us. But we experience indescribable joy when the Source of the universe, which is love, flows through us and out to a suffering world.

As others eat of the fruit in your life, many of them will become seekers, moving through the 3-phased journey of seeking and becoming frustrated, finding and becoming content, and releasing out to others the treasure that you have found.
They too will experience a Divine Wholeness. This is the "holiness" that religion preaches but seldom understands or partakes of.

This wholeness keeps you centered in living the present moment, instead of in thoughts of the past and the future. It also allows you to enjoy things without being attached to them.

It frees your mind from endless chatter and allows creative thoughts to flow from within. It allows you to fully understand that our universe really is one (uni) song (verse) and that we are a part of that harmonious whole.

And so, the game of hide and seek is a game that must be played to its completion. Seek and you will find.

The first thing that you will find is that no/thing outside of yourself can provide what you are seeking. Many give up at this juncture. They surrender to the false notion that they can never be fully content and fulfilled in this life.

The second thing that you will find is frustration because of your seeking. This is a stage, where often we get angry with God. If you read the book of Habbakuk, you see a man who is completely frustrated in the first chapter of that book. He is asking the question "why" over and over.

Many people never press beyond the frustration of this stage. Fortunately, Habbakuk, did. He "entered the stillness long enough to experience a breaking within himself, a separation of his soul and spirit.

But those who yield to the frustration and become aware of the treasure within will find what they were looking for.

And when you find, the seeking is no longer needed. You are no longer a seeker. You have entered a realm of awareness where there is no lack. You then enter wholeness as you release out to others the peace and joy that you have found.

As we progress through this book, you will become aware of the fact that you are not who you thought you were! The real you is not the false ego created by your thoughts, your possessions, your accomplishments, your profession, nor the labels put on you by yourself and others.

The real you is revealed as you enter the Kingdom, through alignment, into the peace, and joy that was there all the time, within you.

The seeker is the caterpillar. The cocoon is the necessary process. The butterfly emerges, never to crawl again.

IN THE QUIET
darrell scott

In the quiet, I find peace, where the outside noises cease

When my mind has settled down, and my thoughts no longer race
In the chambers of my spirit, I have found a secret place

There the unseen things embrace us, the invisible that's real
And we there enjoy the treasures, that activity would steal

Hear the whisper of the poets, who have beckoned us to know
Of that inner sanctuary, where we seldom ever go

In the quiet of our being, creativity is born
And it rises to the surface, to a world that's hurt and torn

Deep within me, love replaces, all the anger and the fear
In the stillness is a "knowing", who I AM and why I'm here

Chapter 3
WHAT IS TRUE RIGHTEOUSNESS?

By now you are probably thinking, "What is this "alignment" business that he keeps writing about?" In previous chapters I have substituted the word "alignment" for the word "righteousness". You will also see me substitute the word "Source" for "God" in this book.

The reason I do that is not to be disrespectful of scripture, but because certain words create images in the mind of the reader that are often dictated by previous doctrine or belief systems. As Shakespeare wisely wrote, "*A rose by any other name would smell as sweet*". In essence, he was saying that a rose is still a rose no matter what you call it.

Sometimes words that are used repeatedly by generations of people become contaminated and lose their meaning. For example, when the word "God" is used over and over again, it creates thought images to different people.

Some may think of an old man with a beard up beyond the clouds on a golden throne. Others may think of a harsh judgmental Being who is watching us like a hawk to punish our misdeeds. Some think of a universal, impersonal "isness". Others may think of a loving invisible Being that is looking for ways to encourage and protect us.

When I use the word "Source" it is simply to realign our thinking with a fresh image, instead of the one that automatically pops into our heads when we use the word "God". God is the Source of everything. I could just as easily use the word life, love, or light, for God is referred to as all of those.

I am also using the word "alignment" instead of "righteousness" Righteousness means we come into an alignment with our soul and spirit that results in wholeness. Paul wrote about this in Romans 6:19 (NIV), where he says, "*righteousness leading to holiness*". This is alignment which leads to wholeness!

26

I believe I am helping us return to the original meaning rather than the one that 2,000 years of religious teaching has given us.

In Hebrew poetry words are commonly paralleled with similar meaning words, such as in the following passage.

> *Be glad in the LORD, and rejoice, O <u>righteous</u>, and shout for joy, all you <u>upright</u> in heart!* (Psalm 32:11 RSV)

The Hebrew words *tsadiyq*, translated as righteous, and *yashar*, (Strong's #3477), translated as upright, are paralleled many times in the Bible indicating that in the Hebrew mind they were similar in meaning.

Upright is another abstract word but it is used in a concrete manner, such as in Jeremiah 31:9, where it means "straight" as in a straight path.

When John the Baptist came on the scene he quoted the prophet Isaiah saying, *"Prepare ye the way of the Lord, make his paths straight. Every valley shall be filled and every mountain and hill shall be brought low; and the crooked shall be made straight, and rough ways shall be made smooth"* (Luke 3:4-6 KJV). John, quoting Isaiah, then says, *"And all flesh shall see the salvation of God".*

There is a lot in these few verses to illuminate, but I want to focus on the first part. The picture being painted here by both John the Baptist and Isaiah is one of alignment. Bringing the high low and the low high. Making the crooked straight and the rough smooth.

All of this is to prepare a straight path, which they call *"the way of the Lord"*. Once there is an alignment, creating a straight path - - then all flesh shall see the salvation of God! Isaiah actually says something that John the Baptist left out when he quoted this. Isaiah said, *"And the glory of the Lord shall be revealed"*.

27

This is a principle of truth that applies to you and to me. When your soul and spirit have been separated (as we shall see later), and the soul (will, emotions, and intellect) have come into alignment with the spirit, a straight path has been created.

A path of righteousness. A path of straightness. A path of alignment. As a result of your individual alignment, you shall see the salvation of God and the glory of the Lord will be revealed - - to and through you!

Isaiah elaborates on this pathway of alignment in another place when he said, *"And a highway will be there; it will be called the Way of Holiness; it will be for those who walk on that Way. The unclean will not journey on it; wicked fools will not go about on it"* (Isaiah 35:8 NIV).

This alignment is referred to again in Matthew 7:14 (KJV): *"Because strait is the gate, and narrow is the way, that leadeth unto life, and few there be that find it"*.

So, putting these verses all together we see an alignment occurring that creates a straight path, or way, that leads to *LIFE - - NOT HEAVEN!* Remember that Jesus said, *"I came that they may have life, and have it abundantly"*.

This straight path is called, "The way of the Lord". And we are encouraged to "Prepare it", i.e. *"Prepare ye the way of the Lord"*. We will come back to how to prepare the way of the Lord shortly.

Now let's look at the word "righteousness" from scripture and see how it is used and how the above verses apply. First, it is important to see that righteousness can be understood from different viewpoints, all of which create the straight path that leads to life.

There is a **_gift_** of righteousness, there is the **_fruit_** of righteousness, and there is a **_harvest_** of righteousness, all of which are seen in the following scriptures.

*"For if, by the trespass of the one man, death reigned through that one man, how much more will those who receive God's abundant provision of grace and of the **gift of righteousness** reign in life through the one man, Jesus Christ"* (Romans 5:17 NIV)

*"And the **fruit of righteousness** is sown in peace of them that make peace."* (James 3:18 NIV)

*"No discipline seems pleasant at the time, but painful. Later on, however, it produces a **harvest of righteousness** and peace for those who have been trained by it."* (Hebrews 12:11 NIV)

For example, many who have received the gift of righteousness do not display the fruit of righteousness. Nor have they produced a harvest of righteousness. The question must be raised at that point - - are they righteous?

If they have not *"exercised their spiritual senses by reason of use"* (Hebrews 5:14) and they have not been *"trained by it"*(Hebrews 12:11), then the answer is "NO". They are *"holding the truth in unrighteousness"* (Romans 1:18 KJV). They are redeemed, but not aligned!

So, I want to take the liberty of substituting the word alignment in place of the word righteousness. We have received a gift of alignment from God. This gift of alignment enables us to produce the fruit of that alignment and provide a harvest resulting from that alignment. The gift is given, the fruit is grown, and the harvest is gathered. This completes the 3 phases of spiritual growth which progressively produce righteousness, peace, and joy!

But, it begins with the gift. And the gift is given freely to everyone. However, it is activated through faith and revealed through faithfulness.

Look closely at the words of Paul and you will see that everyone has received the gift of righteousness:

"For if, by the trespass of the one man, death reigned through that one man, **how much more will those who receive God's abundant provision of grace and of the gift of righteousness reign in life through the one man, Jesus Christ***!*

Consequently, just as one trespass resulted in condemnation for all people, so also **one righteous act resulted in justification and life for all people.** *For just as through the disobedience of the one man the many were made sinners, so also through the obedience of the one man the many will be made righteous".* (Romans 5:17-19 NIV)

The gift of righteousness, or re-alignment with God's purposes was given to everyone through Christ. One righteous act resulted in justification and life for all people (see the verses above). One act of obedience will result in all being made righteous (see the verses above).

Don't get hung up on the words *"the many"*. Those words are applied to all who were made sinners by the disobedience of Adam as well, and that is everyone.

So whoever was made sinners (everyone) through Adam's disobedience, the same (everyone) will be made righteous through Christ's obedience! You may have to go back and reread the verses a few times, but an honest appraisal can provide no other conclusion.

We were completely out of alignment with the Source of our being through the disobedience of Adam. *"We all like sheep have gone astray, each of us has turned to our own way"* (Isaiah 53:6 NIV).

We have strayed from God's purposes and ways and created crooked paths of our own making. Our lives became a series of mountains and valleys, crooked paths, and rough places.

What caused us to stray from the way that leads to life? The answer is simple: Our thoughts, or our minds.

If you go back to the story of Adam and Eve in the garden, the serpent deceived Eve through her thoughts, ultimately causing them to be cast out of the garden. Listen to Paul describe what happened then and what happens to us:

"But I am afraid that just as Eve was deceived by the serpent's cunning, your minds may somehow be led astray" (II Corinthians 11:3 NIV).

So, our thoughts are the culpert that took us away from the alignment with God and his purposes.

The first step in preparing the way of the Lord is to ***receive*** the gift of righteousness so that we can reign in life (not in the future, but now).

Let's look at it again: " - - *how much more will those who **receive** God's abundant provision of grace and of the gift of righteousness reign in life through the one man, Jesus Christ"*.

It is given to everyone, but it is activated by receiving it! As we receive the gift of righteousness, it will begin to work in us to bring forth the fruit of righteousness resulting in a harvest of righteousness. But first things first.

Once the gift of alignment (we are now right with God) has been received, we must begin to bring every mountain in our life down, raising every low place, straightening out the crooked, and smoothing out the rough.

This cannot happen through self-effort, however. It is a work of the spirit. *"For it is God who works in you to will and to act in order to fulfill his good purpose"* (Philippians 2:13 NIV).

We must remember that the gift and fruit of righteousness are both of God, not ourselves. He gives us both the desire and ability to fulfill His good purpose.

So, how do we "prepare the way of the Lord"? By making His paths straight. And how do we do that? By receiving, or acknowledging the gift of alignment.

We must then allow the working of the spirit within us to bring every mountain, valley, and crooked place into alignment with the spirit.

This begins with a realignment of our thought life. This is the point where we were led astray. That is why *we take captive every thought to make it obedient to Christ* (II Corinthians 10:5). So how do we take every thought captive?

It is our thoughts that are the vehicles of all our problems. Worry, stress, depression, condemnation, accusation, deception, judgment of others, gossip, and temptation are all products of thought. Satan is referred to in scripture as the deceiver, the accuser of the brethren, the tempter, etc., all dealing with our thought life.

Since our thoughts are not His thoughts (Isaiah 55:8), and our ways are not His ways, then there must come an adjustment, or alignment of our thoughts and ways with His. How does that occur?

It begins in stillness and in learning to quiet your mind and thoughts. The spirit is always speaking in a still, small voice, but the soul, even of believers, needs restoring and the mind needs renewing. So the noise created by the mind, which is part of the soul, prevents us from hearing the voice of the spirit.

The "how to" of quieting the mind and thoughts will be dealt with in further chapters, but it is important to see that alignment is necessary before we can produce the fruit and project a harvest of righteousness.

The Kingdom of God, which is within you, is described as righteousness (alignment), peace, and joy. The alignment (rightness with God) leads to peace, and the peace leads to joy. The joy (of the Lord) is our strength which leads to power, which leads to authority.

We rule and reign with Him, not just in the future, but in the present as well. For we are seated with him in heavenly places. Where is that? On the throne of his Kingdom which is within us!

Chapter 4
YOU'RE NOT WHO YOU THINK YOU ARE

There is a false 'you' that was created from your own thoughts at an early age, and has enlarged and developed over the years. This great pretender, that you think is 'you', has robbed the real 'you' of your rightful identity and inheritance. You are not the product of your thoughts. You are a spirit being having a human experience, not a human being having spiritual experiences.

We have already seen that your human spirit is the candle of the Lord. That is your true identity. It is the divine part of you, the eternal "I AM" that animates through your soul and body. You *have* a natural body and a natural mind, but you *are* a spiritual being with a spiritual mind. This is clearly confirmed in scripture.

"If there is a natural body, there is also a spiritual body" (I Cor. 15:44 NIV)

"For to be carnally minded is death; but to be spiritually minded is life and peace. Because the carnal mind is enmity against God; for it is not subject to the law of God, neither indeed can it be" (Romans 8:6-7 KJV)

Human thoughts originate from the carnal, or fleshly mind. Spiritual thoughts originate from the spiritual mind, or the mind of Christ. It was our human thoughts that created the image of who we think we are. So there are two sources of our thinking. Like two fountains that merge together at the same place, often we have mixture in our thinking.

"With the tongue we praise our Lord and Father, and with it we curse men, who have been made in God's likeness. Out of the same mouth come praise and cursing. My brothers, this should not be.

Can both fresh water and salt water flow from the same spring? My brothers, can a fig tree bear olives, or a grapevine bear figs? Neither can a salt spring produce fresh water.

34

Who is wise and understanding among you? Let him show it by his good life, by deeds done in the humility that comes from wisdom.

But if you harbor bitter envy and selfish ambition in your hearts, do not boast about it or deny the truth. Such "wisdom" does not come down from heaven but is earthly, unspiritual, of the devil.

For where you have envy and selfish ambition, there you find disorder and every evil practice. But the wisdom that comes from heaven is first of all pure; then peace-loving, considerate, submissive, full of mercy and good fruit, impartial and sincere" (James 3:9-17 NIV)

In these verses, James is describing two sources of thought and wisdom. One is earthly and one is spiritual. So, simply changing negative 'earthly' thoughts into 'earthly' positive thoughts is not enough. All earthly thinking is 'wood, hay, and stubble'. All spiritual thinking is 'gold, silver, and precious stones'.

Many people, even after spiritual awakening, continue to think earthly thoughts from a carnal mind, so they remain unfulfilled and often miserable. They have received the gift of alignment (righteousness), but have not allowed the gift to produce the fruit of alignment.

Some have learned to think spiritually, but still mix in their own earthly thoughts. A few have learned how to walk in the spirit and think from their spiritual mind.

This is when the fruit of righteousness is expressed. Those who walk in the spirit have a peace that passes understanding and a joy that they are not able to describe, because it is unspeakable joy.

The human soul, consisting of will, emotions, and intellect is the source of earthly wisdom. The spirit is the source of spiritual wisdom. So the imposter that we believe we are, is a product of the soul, called the ego.

The soul is not the ego, but the soul creates the ego. The ego is created through thought *by attachment* to things, i.e., opinions, doctrines, people, possessions, popularity, etc. These attachments, through thought, create the false identity of ego.

We were created (spirit) in the image of God (who is Spirit), and yet our human soul creates its own image, the ego. Now there are two fountains of wisdom that strive for dominance; the flesh (soulish ego) and the spirit (candle of the Lord).

A major step to true, lasting fulfillment in life is to recognize that there is a veil created by the "white noise" of your thoughts that separates you from the inner peace and joy that is hidden in your human spirit.

The veil of the human "psyche" must be ripped apart in order for the spirit to flow out freely. That is why Jesus said, *"For whoever wants to save his life (psyche) will lose it, but whoever loses his life (psyche) for me will find it"*(Matthew 16:25 NIV).

The Greek word for "life" in this scripture is "psyche" from which we get the word psychology. It is the exact same word as "soul" found in the next verse: *"What good will it be for a man if he gains the whole world, yet forfeits his **soul** (psyche)"*.

So the verse could read, just as accurately: *"For whoever wants to save his soul will lose it, but whoever loses his soul for me will find it"*. A liberal translation might say, *"For whoever wants to save his mind will lose it - -"*.

There are 3 Greek words in the Bible that are translated into the English word "life". They are *bios*, *psyche*, and *zoe*. We get the word biology from the word bios. Bios is simply our physical life.

We get the word psychology from the word *psyche*. *Psyche* is the human soul which is centered in the mind. We get the word zoology from the word *zoe*. *Zoe*, in scripture is the divine life.

36

It is the word used in connection with eternal life (*aionios zoe*), which should be translated "agelasting life".

The title of this book, <u>Lose Your Mind and Find Your Purpose</u>, came from the words of Jesus, "*Whoever finds their life will lose it, and whoever loses their life for my sake will find it*" (Matthew 10:39 NIV).

This statement has been so misunderstood by so many. If you take it literally, you might think that it is saying to kill yourself so that you can find your life. If the Greek word used here was "*bios*" instead of "*psyche*", then suicide would have been the instruction!

Losing your "*psyche*", your soulish life, is a requirement before you can live the abundant life that Jesus promised. Notice that a different word for life is used in John 10:10 for "life". "*I came that they may have life (zoe), and have it abundantly*".

In losing your psyche (soulish life) you are surrendering to zoe (spiritual life) which then restores your psyche (soul) and renews your mind - - allowing you to find the life of wholeness you wanted.

If you want the spiritual life (*zoe*), then the soulish life (*psyche*) must be surrendered. You must lose one to gain the other. If you want the mind of Christ, you must lose the carnal mind. If you want to think spiritual thoughts, you must abandon soulish thoughts.

The soul (*psyche*) is understood by most theologians to be a compilation of will, emotion, and intellect, all centered in the human mind. All three of these are expressions from the mind. Our will, or the choices we make, are from the mind.

Our emotional reactions originate from our thoughts, or mind. And, of course, all our logic, deductions, analysis, etc. are from the intellectual part of our mind.

This is why there must be a separation of soul and spirit by the living Word, not just the written Word.

It is the spiritual daily bread that gives us fulfillment, not the dead letter of old bread. That is why memorizing scripture is not the answer. Some of the most soulish people I know can quote scripture like a tape recorder.

When we read the words, "Lose your life", we are tempted to allow false religious concepts to guide us down a road of self-denial, legalism and discipline that promotes a life of misery. As my mentor, Bob Mumford, often said, "Don't try to crucify yourself, you'll always use rubber nails!".

Self-crucifixion is not what this book is about. Rather, it is about letting go of all that misery which is connected to an unredeemable "carnal" or "sinful" mind, hostile and not submitted to God's purposes (Romans 8:7).

It is about learning how to observe our thoughts without judging them or being identified with them. It is about detaching completely from those thoughts and rising into a state of awareness from within. Awareness is much more powerful than thought. We cannot be aware of the present moment if we are constantly thinking of the past or future.

Quite simply, it is our thoughts that hold us in bondage. Thoughts cause guilt, shame, despair, unbelief and accusations, as well as, pride, jealousy, envy, and arrogance. When God said that his thought are not our thoughts, he didn't say that his thoughts are some of our thoughts - - he said that the two are completely opposite of each other.

We have believed for too long that we can clean up our thoughts, memorize scripture, or think positive thoughts and somehow through our own effort, transform our minds. But, for those of us who went down that path, eventually we came to realize the futility that resulted.

The answer lies in withdrawing from identification with our human thoughts and entering the still, quiet realm of the spirit.

38

It is letting go of the carnal mind and tapping into the mind of Christ. Then alignment with God and His purposes becomes a reality.

Paul said, *"If we are out of our mind, it is for the sake of God; if we are in our right mind, it is for you"* (II Cor. 5:13 NIV).

We must get out of our mind for the sake of God. In other words, we must still the noise of our natural mind before we can tap into the "right mind", which is the mind of Christ. Then, through righteousness, or alignment with His mind, we can minister life and truth to others.

The "right mind" Paul spoke of is your spiritual mind. It is the source of all true creativity.

We must get out of our old mind and put on the mind of Christ. How do we do this? The answer will continue to unfold, but the first step is to recognize that we have a choice. We can think with the carnal mind as immature "babes in Christ" or we can walk in the spirit with the mind of Christ.

After recognizing that we have a choice, we can detach from our old thought patterns, realizing that our thoughts are not who we are. When the philosopher, Descartes wrote, "I think, therefore I am", he created one of the biggest deceptions of all time. It is exactly the opposite of what he said. I AM, therefore I think.

When the 'I AM' thinks through us we are tapped into the deep, still waters where our soul is restored. Regeneration begins in your spirit. Renewing your mind leads to the process of restoring your soul.

It is not in the thunderous noise of your thinking, nor the whirlwind of your thoughts, nor even the fire of passion from your emotions that you hear God's voice. It is when you detach from the constant chatter of the human mind and move into the inner chambers of your spirit, drinking from the still waters, that your soul is restored.

The Kingdom of God was purposely hidden in the last place we are prone to look for it - - within us. It is when we stop seeking for answers outside of ourselves that we turn to the Source within and find that for which we were seeking.

EGO'S SCAM
darrell scott

Believing that my thoughts are me
Has caused me such confusion
Creating false identity
Resulting in illusion

But yielding to a quiet mind
Exposing ego's scam
By letting go, I've come to know
In stillness - - who I AM

Chapter 5
POSITION VS. CONDITION

Before we get too far, I want to cover some elementary principles that will help us understand why we must lose our mind in order to enter the Kingdom of God, which is a realm of alignment (righteousness), peace, and joy. So - - here we go!

God only sees two people in the world, and those two people are Adam and Christ. Everyone born into this world is born in Adam. When we are "born again", or have a spiritual awakening, we are taken out of Adam and placed in Christ. Scripture is very clear about this.

"For as <u>in Adam</u> all die, even so <u>in Christ</u> shall all be made alive, but each in his own order." I Cor. 15:22

"The first man, Adam, became a living soul. The last Adam became a life-giving spirit. However, the spiritual is not first, but the natural; then the spiritual. The first man is from the earth, earthy; the second man is from heaven. As is the earthy, so also are those that are earthy; and as is the heavenly, so also are those who are heavenly." I Cor 15:45-48

So everyone was born in Adam, and everyone will die in Adam. However, the good news is that *everyone* will be made alive in Christ, but - - *each in his own order*. We are going to refer to these two men as our "position". Our position is either in Adam or in Christ. There is no other position to be in.

It's important to understand that you and I were totally unable to get out of Adam and into Christ through anything we could do.

It was done for us by Christ. The only way out of Adam was through death, and the only way into Christ was through resurrection. Jesus did both for us! He became the *"last Adam"* (see I Cor. 15:45) so that in Him we could die to Adam.

When Christ died at Calvary, we *"died with Him"* (II Tim. 2:11 NAS). Jesus is not called the "second Adam", he is called the *"last Adam"* and the *"second man"*! We don't need a second Adam! As the *"last Adam"* he died for us to escape the *"first Adam"*.

As the *"second man"* he resurrected so that *"in Him we live"* (Acts17:28). He is *"the way, the truth, and the life"*! He is the way out of Adam and the way into resurrected life! This was provided for all humankind. Notice that is says, *"For as in Adam, all die, even so in Christ shall all be made alive"* (I Cor. 15:22). It doesn't say, "In Adam, all die, so in Christ shall a smaller number be made alive", it says "all".

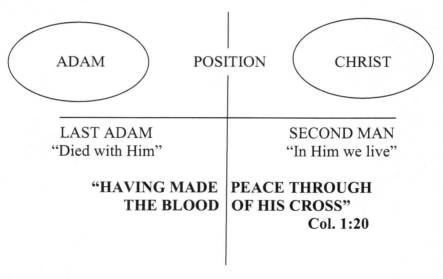

So Jesus, as the "last Adam" died for us in order to take us from Adam into Christ. In Christ as the "second man" we have our new, permanent position! It is important to understand that once you come into Christ, you don't go back and forth from Adam to Christ.

Because we were born in Adam, we received an inheritance from Adam called "the flesh". In essence, "the flesh" (Gk. "sarx") is a combination of our body and soul. The body relates to the world through the 5 senses of touch, taste, hearing, seeing, and smelling.

The soul is expressed through our will, emotions, and intellect. Every believer and nonbeliever, as long as they live, have this inheritance from Adam called "the flesh".

However, when we were awakened, we received a new inheritance from Christ called "the spirit". Our body was not born again, and our soul was not born again. It was our spirit that experienced a rebirth. Jesus said to Nicodemus (John 3:6 NAS) *"That which is born of the flesh is flesh, and that which is born of the Spirit is spirit."*

If a person is 17 years old when their spirit is quickened to life, they have 17 years of habit patterns that have been developed by the body and soul, the flesh. Their spirit is a new and unfamiliar component.

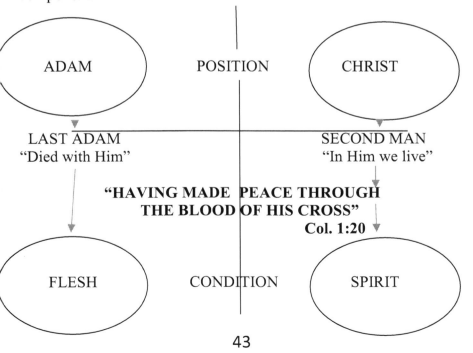

For us to live in freedom, peace, and joy, we must learn to live from spirit and not from our old soulish ways. But because we have acquired a lifetime of soulish habits, responses, and ways of thinking, a struggle begins to take place between the two.

This creates a lot of frustration because we are torn between the desires of the flesh and the new inspirations of the spirit. This is seen in Gal. 5:17 (NAS) *"For the flesh sets its desire against the Spirit, and the Spirit against the flesh; for these are in opposition to one another, so that you may not do the things that you please."*

From our natural birth, **our position** was in Adam, and **our condition** was that we walked in the flesh. We could not walk in the spirit while we were in Adam. However, once we are awakened, our new position is in Christ, which enables us to walk in, or live from, the spirit.

We still have the inheritance we received from Adam, called "the flesh", but we now have a new inheritance as well, called "the spirit". The inheritance was there all the time, in everyone, but the awakening gave us access to it.

So the challenge for us is to learn to walk and live in the spirit, not in the flesh! Our position never changes in Christ, but our condition can fluctuate between living from the flesh and living from the spirit.

What this really boils down to is whether we are thinking and living from our human mind, or from the mind of Christ. Until we completely lose the first one, we cannot completely live our lives guided by the second one.

Now, even though there are only two men in the world, Adam and Christ, there are three *types* of people! I know how confusing that sounds, but it will become clear when we look at the next chart.

Chapter 6
THREE TYPES OF PEOPLE

Although there are only two men in the world, Adam and Christ, there are three types of people in the world. They are: The NATURAL man, the CARNAL man, and the SPIRITUAL man. (This is not a gender thing, and applies to both men and women. I am just using the Biblical word "man").

Let's take a look at the natural man first. The natural man (or woman) is in Adam, positionally, and is living from the flesh, conditionally. The natural man does not have a choice. He *cannot* live in the spirit.

Since he cannot live in the spirit, he does not have access to the treasures of the Kingdom: Righteousness, peace, and joy. Until a spiritual awakening happens, he, or she, is completely blind to the riches that God has placed inside their human spirit.

"But the natural man receiveth not the things of the Spirit of God: for they are foolishness unto him: neither can he know them, because they are spiritually discerned." I Cor. 2:14 (KJV)

When we were in Adam, before we were awakened, we could not understand the depth of spiritual truths. It wasn't difficult - - it was impossible! The natural man cannot receive the things of the Spirit.

Spiritual principles made no sense to us, because we did not have the desire, nor ability to comprehend them. We were in Adam, walking in the flesh as a natural person. We thought our own thoughts through our natural mind, not realizing that our thoughts are not His thoughts, and our ways are not His ways.

Our soul was totally in control of our life, leaving us tossed around by outer circumstances, instead of being governed by peace from within.

We sought for answers outside of ourselves, but all in vain. We thought a better home or car was what would bring happiness. We looked for answers through education, politics, sports, religion, entertainment, and organizations. But no matter how much we looked outside ourselves, the answers alluded us.

We were caught in the trap of the U2 song, "*I have climbed highest mountains, I have run through fields, I have run, I have crawled, I have scaled the city walls. But I still haven't found what I'm looking for*".

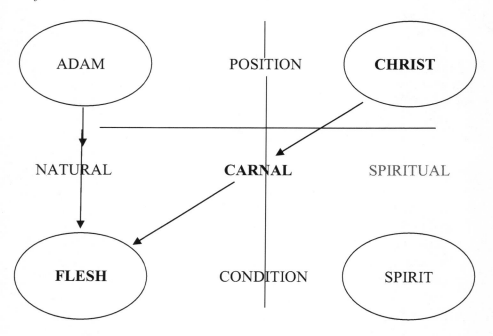

Our spiritual awakening brought us out of Adam and into Christ. Now we have the ability to, not only walk in the flesh, but to also walk in the spirit! We still have our soul and body (the flesh), but we also have an awakened spirit.

However, since we are a spiritual baby, we have not yet learned how to walk in the spirit. We have been walking in the flesh for a long time.

We have developed habit patterns and thought patterns that now are being challenged by our spiritual senses and by the Word of God.

So although we have awakened, we are not yet mature spiritually. However, we are no longer natural. Remember the natural man is in Adam, and we are no longer there.
Paul uses a term to describe those who are in Christ, but are walking in the flesh. That term is the "carnal man". The second *kind* of person is the "carnal man".

"And I - - - could not speak unto you as unto spiritual, but as unto carnal, even as unto babes in Christ." II Cor. 3:1 (KJV)

After spiritual awakening you are no longer "natural". The natural man and the carnal man may appear the same because of their actions, but one is in Adam and one is in Christ. The person who is carnal is still thinking and acting out of their old habit patterns. They have not yet ceased from their own thoughts and ways.

If you are in Christ, you are either carnal or spiritual. You are either "walking in the flesh" or you are "walking in the spirit". There is nothing wrong with being carnal when you are newly awakened. It's normal. It is the phase of babyhood in which the spirit is intended to learn, grow, and produce fruit.

However, if you have been spiritually awakened for 10 years and you are still carnal, something is very wrong!

No one expects a newborn baby to drive a car, read a book, or write an essay. Babies are expected to cry, eat, and create dirty diapers. And yet, too often, religion expects spiritual babies to immediately be mature! Religion, unfortunately, destroys some of its newborn because of unrealistic expectations. Newborns need to be loved, nourished, and cleaned up when they mess up.

But, with time, and right instruction, impartation, etc., one begins to learn *how* to walk in the spirit. There is a period of transition that takes one from the carnal walk to the spiritual walk.

47

Paul writes about those who "by reason of use have their (spiritual) senses exercised (Heb. 5:14).

It is important to understand that once we come out of Adam and into Christ, our former position is forever gone. It is also important to understand that we will never be "natural" again.

The carnal man may look and act natural but he is not. Natural is no longer a choice. You are either in a carnal condition or a spiritual condition.

Charts can never fully explain the mysteries of the spirit, but I am using this insufficient set of charts to help point the reader to the right direction, so that you may have somewhat of an understanding of the differences.

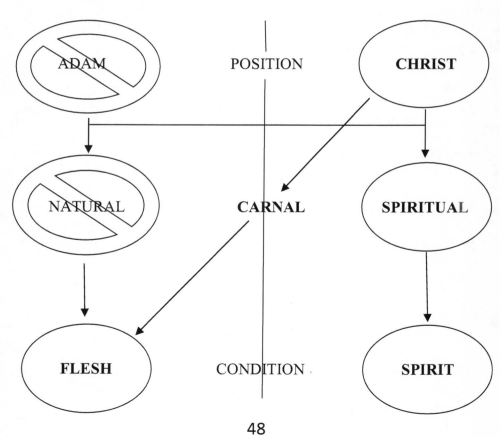

There is only one position for a spiritually awakened person, and that is: "in Christ". However, there are two areas of condition: "the flesh" and "the spirit".

We now have a choice. We can either choose to walk in the flesh or we can choose to walk in the spirit. We are "in Christ" positionally regardless of which condition we find ourselves in.

Now, let's look closer at the origin and definition of these two men. The first Adam was made a "living soul (Gk. psyche)" while the second man was made a "quickening spirit (Gk. pneuma)". So, through the cross, Jesus died as the last of Adam. Through the open tomb, he rose as the second man. This is the order of our progression: Die to soul, live in spirit.

Therefore, Jesus said that whoever saves, or perserves his soul (Gk. psyche) will lose it, and whoever loses his soul, will find it. We must lose our old mind, and way of thinking, in exchange for the "mind of Christ".

God said, *"For my thoughts are not your thoughts, neither are your ways my ways"* (Isaiah 55:8). He did not say, "My thoughts are not some of your thoughts" or even "most of your thoughts". He said that his thoughts are not our thoughts - - period.

So, our "old man" was crucified with him, but too often we are still thinking from our old mind, and that old mind is dead - - producing nothing but dead works. *"For to be carnally minded is death; but to be spiritually minded is life and peace"* (Romans 8:6).

So, before we get bogged down with too much theological yadda yadda, I want to lay out a simple premise, confirmed by scripture, that shows you how to live a life of true alignment, or righteousness, peace, and joy, by losing your mind.

All of the answers that we seek are already within us, waiting for discovery. It is the human mind that creates a veil of separation between God's thoughts and ours.

We can learn, through quieting the human mind, how to listen to the still small voice of spirit within us.

The Divine Source never stops speaking - - we just can't hear because of the outer noises that bombard our ears, and the white noise of our own thoughts.

The chapters that follow will address the steps necessary to lose our natural mind and acquire a "renewed mind" of spirit that "overcomes the world". The end result will be a sense of alignment (righteousness), resulting in peace, and joy that never leaves us nor forsakes us.

SOUL and SPIRIT
darrell scott

Soul and spirit aren't the same, as so many do declare
And although they're both invisible, big differences are there

One is Source and one expression, one the thinker, one the thought
One eternal, one but fleeting, one the teacher, one the taught

Mind, emotions, and volition, all components of the soul
Meant as servants to the spirit, as they each express their role

But the spirit of a lion, and the meekness of a lamb
Lie beneath in quiet stillness, the Eternal, Great I AM

Chapter 7
SEPARATION OF SOUL AND SPIRIT

In my opinion, the most important overlooked truth in the Bible is the subject of separation of soul and spirit.

"For the word of God is living and active. Sharper than any double-edged sword, it penetrates even to dividing soul and spirit - -" Hebrews 4:12 NIV

Unfortunately, most people believe that they are two-dimensional beings: the visible body, and the invisible soul, or spirit, which they believe are the same thing. However, it is very clear in scripture that there is a difference between soul and spirit.

The great Chinese Christian writer, Watchman Nee, defined the soul as the human will, emotion, and intellect, while defining the spirit as intuition, conscience, and communion. The truth is, as Nee admitted, no definition is good enough to describe the complexities of soul and spirit. However, he gave us some good parameters to begin with.

In I Thess. 5:23 (KJV) it says, *"May your whole spirit, soul, and body be kept blameless at the coming of our Lord Jesus Christ"*.

The Greek and Hebrew words for soul and spirit are completely different. For example in the original Greek wording of the New Testament "soul" was "psyche" while "spirit" was "pnuema".

Remember the verses we read concerning Jesus and Adam in the last chapter? The first man, **Adam**, was made a living **soul**, while the second man, **Jesus**, was made a life-giving **spirit**. When we walk in the "flesh" as a carnal person, we are being "soulish".

When we walk in the spirit we are being "spiritual". So our goal should be to learn how to walk in the spirit, and that's why this book was written.

What does this mean for you on a normal day-to-day application? It means that either you live as a victim of your thoughts and emotions, tossed around by your circumstances, or you live in peace and joy regardless of outer situations.

This is not just theory - - it is real in my life and the lives of many others. We will never fulfill the purpose for which we were born if we do not experience a separation of these two invisible components of our existence.

Once we understand that the spirit and soul are not the same thing, and that God wants to divide, or separate them with the sword of the spirit, we need to understand the function of each.

Let's look at a few verses that help us understand the spirit better:

"The spirit of man is the candle of the Lord" Psalms 20:27 KJV

"But it is a spirit in a man, the breath of the Almighty, that gives him understanding." Job 32:8 NIV

"That which is born of the flesh is flesh; and that which is born of the Spirit is spirit" John 3:6 KJV

"God is a Spirit: and they that worship him must worship him in spirit and in truth." John 4:24 KJV

"For they that are after the flesh do mind the things of the flesh; but they who are after the spirit the things of the spirit." Romans 8:5 KJV

"The Spirit himself testifies with our spirit that we are God's children."   Romans 8:16 NIV

Let me recap what the above verses all say about the spirit. The human spirit is the candle of the Lord. It is the spirit in us, not the soul, that gives understanding. That which is born of Spirit, is not soul, but spirit. We must worship God in spirit.

We must mind the things of spirit. God's spirit testifies with our spirit - - - not soul, that we are the children of God.

The spirit within us is a piece of the Divine Source, the I AM that desires to express itself through our soul and body. He is the light that lights every man that comes into the world (John 1:9 KJV) because the spirit of man is the candle of the Lord.

The soul is the part of us that Jesus said we must lose in order to find it. The spirit is what is reborn in us, but according to Psalm 23 it is the soul that needs to be restored. It is the soul that needs saving: James 1:21. It is the soul that needs purifying: I Peter 1:22. The reawakened spirit is the beginning of our journey, but the end of our salvation is the salvation of our souls: I Peter 1:9.

So, a very important step in our spiritual growth and maturity is allowing the word of God to separate our soul from our spirit. For those who have experienced this, hearing the Divine Inner Voice becomes much easier.

They learn the difference between soulish and spiritual thoughts and activities. The separation of soul and spirit brings us into the "rest" spoken of in Hebrews, where we cease from our (soulish) labor and enter God's (spiritual) rest.

If you read Hebrews chapters 3 and 4 you will find the subject of "stopping our own works and entering into God's rest". The word "rest" is used 11 times in those two chapters.

The reason that Israel did not occupy the Promised Land of Canaan sooner was because of one simple thing: unbelief. God had promised them a land flowing with milk and honey, wells they didn't dig, vineyards they didn't plant, and houses they didn't build.

What a powerful group of promises! And yet, it took them 40 years to travel between Egypt and the Promised Land when it should have taken them 40 days.

But unbelief was the reason they failed. Unbelief is the result of human thinking. The promises were real, but the physical obstacles caused them to think that they could not receive the promises. They saw giants in the land of Canaan and their logic told them that they were not strong enough to occupy the land promised to them.

I have read commentaries by theologians about those giants and what they represent, but we don't need to focus on the giants. The giants were never the problem. It was their minds - - their thought processes - - that prevented them from entering the land.

They needed to lose their stinkin' thinkin' and withdraw from their minds into their spirits where God's promises rang true. They needed a "head transplant".

David didn't worry about the size of Goliath or his armor. He focused on what he was hearing in his spirit and ignored the thoughts of his brothers and of Saul, who were all logically thinking that there was no way a small boy could kill a fully armed giant with nothing more than a slingshot.

We are warned in Hebrews 4 that we can fail to attain the "rest" that we were promised because of the same problem: unbelief. This is not talking about "losing our salvation" or some future reward or punishment. It says, *"Today, if you hear his voice, do not harden your hearts"* (Hebrews 4:3).

How much clearer can the writer of Hebrews make it? Today you can enter God's rest and cease from your own sweat and effort, entering His Kingdom of alignment, peace, and joy.

Do you really want to live in total peace and experience joy every day of your life, even when things fall apart in the world around you? That may seem impossible to you at the moment, but I can promise you that it is available and real to you right now, if you will have ears to hear what I am saying.

Following this entire discourse about "entering into rest" we read this verse: *"For the word of God is living and active. Sharper than any double -edged sword, it penetrates even to dividing soul and spirit - -"* Hebrews 4:12 NIV

The sword that separates soul and spirit is the word of God. However, it is not the written word that does the work, it is the living, current, proceeding word of God that does the separation. There are some who believe that after the Bible was written, God quit speaking.

Jesus said, *"It is written, Man shall not live by bread alone, but by every word that proceedeth out of the mouth of God"* (Matthew 4:4 KJV). It is the fresh, living word that separates soul and spirit.

Jesus also said for us to pray and ask the Father to give us *this* day our daily bread. If you study the history of the Bible you will find that for the first 60 years after Christ's resurrection the believers had no New Testament.

And yet, they continued to hear and obey the voice of the Lord, even though there was no book of Acts, Romans, or Ephesians. They were not dependent on the Bible, because they didn't have one!

In Hebrews 3:7 it says, *"So, as the Holy Spirit says; 'Today if you hear his voice, do not harden your hearts"*. If we harden our hearts by refusing to hear and respond to the inner voice of God today, we will lose our ability to hear. Millions of people read the Bible daily, but never hear the voice of the Lord speaking to them.

Over and over, Jesus said, "He that has an ear to hear - - let him hear".

The rest of this book is about that sword, the living, current word of God bringing a separation between our soul (Gk. psyche) and our spirit (Gk. pnuema). We will then be able to recognize when our words and actions are 'soulish' or 'spiritual'.

We can learn to live in peace and joy in our spirit even when our soul is in turmoil and our body is in pain. It is peace that "passes understanding" because it makes no sense.

Chapter 8
BE STILL - - AND KNOW

"Be still and know that I am God" (Psalm 46:10). God did not say, "Study much and know that I am God". He did not say, "Listen to sermons and know that I am God". He did not say, "Have great experiences and know that I am God". He did not say go to services regularly and know that I am God. He said, *"Be still and know"*.

Knowing is crucial to a liberated life. Daniel 11:32 says, *"They that know their God shall be strong and do exploits"*. We are told that we will be strong and do great things once we know God. But we are also told that the primary way to know God is to be still. What does it mean to *"be still"*?

We have looked at the differences between soul and spirit and seen that the soul was meant to express the spirit's thoughts, words, and activities. Unfortunately, the soul wants to be in control, especially in the realm of our thoughts.

In the book of Psalms the words "my soul" are mentioned 105 times. From those scriptures, we see that the soul is "vexed, distressed, in need of deliverance, troubled, needs healing, is cast down, is bowed down, needs redeeming, and is full of troubles".

All of this anxiety, frustration, and depression takes place in the soul. The soul is like the surface of a lake that is being tossed about and lashed by an angry storm, while the spirit is like the depths of the lake that remains still and calm in the midst of the storm.

Therefore, an important part of entering the Kingdom of alignment, peace, and joy, is to quiet down the soul and enter into the stillness of the spirit within you.

David understood this when he wrote in Psalm 131:2, *"Surely I have behaved and quieted myself, as a child that is weaned of his mother: my soul is even as a weaned child."*

58

Like Elijah in the cave, we must wait for the whirlwind, the earthquake, and the fire to settle down before we can hear the still small voice within our spirit.

"This is what the Sovereign LORD, the Holy One of Israel, says: "In repentance and rest is your salvation, in quietness and trust is your strength, but you would have none of it" (Isa. 30:15 NIV).

There are 3 types of repentance talked about in scripture. The word "repentance" means "a turning away from one thing to another". Repentance from sin, a turning away from sin and a turning to obedience. Then there is a repentance from dead works.

Repentance, or "turning away" from dead works is much more subtle than turning away from sin. Soulish prayer, soulish fasting, and soulish Bible reading can all be "dead works".

We think of repentance as a turning away from bad things, but the good things done from wrong motives or desires are "dead works" that we are called to "turn away" from as well. Even good things done with right motives can be "dead works" if they originate from the soul instead of the spirit.

So, just to recap: We are to turn away from sin to obedience. We are to turn away from dead works of the soul to fruit of the spirit.

However, there is a third type of repentance mentioned in the Bible, a repentance, or turning away from, the noise in our life. Turning away from the surface activity and the white noise of our own thoughts to the stillness within us where the Kingdom awaits. You have probably never heard that type of repentance taught or preached in a church service.

"(God says) In repentance and rest is your salvation, in quietness and trust is your strength, but you would have none of it" (Isaiah 30: 15 NIV).

The KJV says, *"In returning"* instead of *"In repentance"*. God challenges us to repent or turn away from the soulish thoughts and activities and enter into his rest - - ceasing from our own labors.

The first part of this chapter, Isaiah 50, describes people who are obstinate, with plans of their own, without consulting Him. It's easy for us to view them as terrible disobedient people, but take a look at your own life.

Have you lived your life with your own plans, not consulting with him? I know that I have at times. That makes you and I the obstinate person He is talking about!

He calls us to repent or return, away from the noise of our own head, and enter His rest! He also warns us that if we choose to flee on horses, he will send others to chase us on faster horses (Isaiah 30:16 NIV).

Have you ever felt God calling you to slow down and enter His stillness, but instead, like Jonah, you ran the other way? Don't worry - - He has a big fish waiting on you. He has horses faster than yours, that will chase you down!

But He doesn't do this to punish you – He does it to purge you. It's your choice. You can fall on the rock and be broken, or the rock can fall on you and grind you to powder (Matthew 21:44).

You get to choose whether you are going to repent and enter rest, stillness, and quietness, where you can hear His voice, or whether you are going to run and be overtaken.

The cool part of this story in Isaiah 30 is that He will wait until you are worn out from running and when you finally decide to cry out to Him, He will answer (verses 18-19). He will then be gracious to you, gently leading you to that place of rest and stillness that He invited you to enter in the first place.

And, although He has given you the "bread of adversity" and the "water of affliction" it was all for your good (verse 20). Notice that it was God, not the devil, who gave us the bread of adversity and the water of affliction.

Too many people are rebuking the devil when they should be learning the lesson God has ordained for them. The simplistic message that all bad things are from the devil and all good things are from God does not hold up to scripture.

It is in quietness and trust that we find strength. Notice that it is in turning away from noise to rest that we find salvation! This is the *"end of your faith, even the salvation of your souls"* (I Peter 1:9 KJV).

"But they that wait upon the Lord shall renew their strength; they shall mount up with wings as eagles; they shall run, and not be weary; and they shall walk and not faint" (Isaiah 40:31 KJV).

"Come to me, all you who are weary and burdened, and I will give you rest" (Matthew 11:28 NIV).

There is a place for prayer and meditation in our lives, but what is being described here is neither prayer, nor meditation. In prayer we are communicating something. In meditation we are thinking about something. Here we detach from both communication and thinking and move into a deeper place of "awareness". This is the Holy of Holies.

This is the "secret place of the Most High". From this place of stillness all creativity is born. It is here that we express spiritual truths in spiritual words (I Cor. 2:13-15). It is here that we discern what is spiritual and what is soulish. It is here that we can judge with a righteous judgment. The masses are "lost in thought", but you can turn away from the surface and enter the powerful stillness that lies beneath your mind, in your spirit. Deep calls unto deep, and spiritual strength waits patiently for you to heed the call and go deeper.

A QUIET PLACE MY KINGDOM IS*

A quiet place, my kingdom is,
And there such pleasures I do find
That far surpass the outward things
That try to captivate my mind
I've learned to live without the things
Desired by royalty and kings

No wealth, no fads that soon will fade
No risky game that brings a thrill
No shiny toys, no fancy clothes
They all will slowly lose appeal
And as my thoughts begin to cease
I find a place of perfect peace

I see the wealthy unfulfilled
And hasty climbers often fall
And those who choose to act so proud
Become the biggest fools of all
They gain by toil, They keep by fear
Their smile devoid of any cheer

I find contentment is my goal
While others wallow in their greed
I realize that outward things
Can never meet my deepest need
I now live inward like a king
Content with what awareness brings

Some have too much, and crave for more
A hunger that will never end
I have not much, but live in peace
Content with what I have within
They're poor, I'm rich, They beg, I give
They slowly die, I daily live

I laugh not at another's loss
I envy not another's gain
For I'm connected to the Source
And live in peace that few attain
I fear no foe, I flatter none
And I will live 'till life is done

Some find their pleasure through their lust
While others rule by stubborn will
In gold and silver is their trust
While some seek purpose through a thrill
But all the treasure that I find
Is found beneath a quiet mind

My health and ease are all I need
A conscience clear of all deceit
No bribe nor threat to taint my deed
An honest pathway for my feet
It's how I live, It's how I'll die
I wish that all could do as I

*Darrell Scott reworded a poem by Edward Dyer in 1588 titled, "My Mind to Me a Kingdom Is"

There is nothing wrong with enjoying things such as cars, planes, houses, and wealth. However, if those things control our lives, and we seek our joy and peace from them, we will be greatly disappointed. We enjoy them the most when we are detached from them.

Attachment to any "thing" blocks the flow of the Kingdom. For me, the practice of detaching from, and observing my thoughts started in the shower. As I began to realize the importance of quieting my mind and listening to my spirit, I started practicing that every morning in the shower.

It became such an experience of bliss that I would selfishly stand there until all the hot water was used up.

Needless to say, my wonderful wife, Sandy, was not all that pleased with my lengthy spiritual encounters, so I had to continue that practice outside the shower throughout the day.

SACRED SHOWER
darrell scott

The shower is my sacred place
Where water cascades down my face
And yielding to its warm embrace
My anxious thoughts can cease

And slowly I begin to see
The "being" that is really me
Immersed beneath this liquid sea
A Presence full of peace

My thoughts now lose their strength and force
And yielding to a deeper Source
They recognize a better course
Where only Presence goes

Awareness now replaces thought
And mental battles I have fought
I realize were all for naught
As Presence slowly grows

I find that "being" supersedes
My racing thoughts and active deeds
Replacing all my outer needs
With inward gentle power

Amazingly, this healing grace
Is always there for my embrace
And can be found at anyplace
Not just inside the shower

Places that are considered pagan to some, are viewed as sacred to others. To Catholics, the Basilica of St. Francis and the Sistine Chapel are sacred places. To Protestants it may be a trip to Jerusalem or their home church. To Mormons it may be the Temple in Salt Lake City.

Muslims regard Mecca and Medina as holy sites. To Buddhists, it may be Lumbini, the birthplace of the Buddha. To Hindus, the Ganges River, to Jews, the Western, or "Wailing Wall", and to Wiccans it may be Stonehenge.

These places are considered sacred, for the most part, because of their history or because of a belief system that creates a strong bond between the person and that particular place.

Then there are places or occurrences in nature, such as rainbows, waterfalls, sunsets, secluded beaches, magnificent rainforests, etc. that also become sacred places for those who experience them.

However, as the poem points out, there is a sacred place within each of us. We have the ability to find our sacred place regardless of where we are.

My daughter, Rachel, wrote an article about this sacred place within while on a rafting trip. It was a month before she was killed at Columbine High School.

She ended her writing by saying, *"Wherever I go, I will find sanctuary"*. We are not limited to spiritual engagement by geographic locations. Find the sanctuary within you, wherever you go.

Christ warned of the folly of seeking the Kingdom outside of ourselves. He admonished us not to look "here or there", but to look within. He said, "For the Kingdom of Heaven is within you".

Wherever you may be, in the shower, or in dense traffic, you can chose to dip beneath the white noise of your turbulent, never-ending thoughts and enter the calm, deep waters within.   This reservoir of stillness, peace, and freedom is undisturbed by all that is on the surface.

"The calm within the storm is where peace lives and breathes. It is not within perfect circumstances or a charmed life - - it is not conditional. Peace is a sacred space within. It is the temple of our internal landscape. We are free to visit it, whenever we seek sanctuary. Underneath the chaos of everyday living, peace is patiently awaiting our discovery - - go within." Jaeda DeWalt

Chapter 9
WHO IS MY ENEMY?

*"Know your enemy and know yourself and you
can fight a hundred battles without disaster"*
General Sun Tzu (ancient military strategist)

When David fought Goliath he was not being cocky or foolishly brave when he rejected Saul's armor. He understood that to take on this monstrous giant, he would have to be wise in his strategy and weapon selection. Goliath was weighted down with heavy armor, a shield, and a spear. This would slow him down considerably.

David knew that Saul's armor was too heavy for him and would hinder his flexibility and ability to maneuver. He also knew that he was not skilled at using a spear or sword. So, he chose to use a weapon that would give him maximum advantage: his slingshot. He had proven his skill with that weapon when ferocious lions and bears attempted to attack the sheep in his care. He had killed them all.

David understood that the weapons and armor of Goliath would slow him down, so his strategy was simple: Stay flexible, mobile, and use the weapon he had proven to be successful against large, aggressive enemies, such as lions and bears.

Understanding his enemy's strengths, weaknesses, weapons, and strategy and confidence in his own strategy, weapon, and skills brought David the victory. And most importantly, he had confidence that God was directing his efforts.

It has been often stated by experienced generals and warriors, that the better you understand your enemy, the better chance you have for victory. 3 things are very important to know, about your enemy when engaging warfare. Who is the enemy? What are his weapons? What are his strategies? You need to know these 3 things about yourself as well.

Most Christians would say that their enemy is an entity called the devil, Satan, the evil one, the serpent, and many other descriptive words. But few understand the enemy's weapons and strategy. First let's take a closer look at who our enemy is. Then we will look at understanding his weapons and strategy. The entity we call "the devil" is called a liar (John 8:44 NIV), a deceiver (Rev. 20:8 KJV), a tempter (I Thess. 3:5 KJV), and an accuser (Rev. 12:10 NIV).

He is not only called a liar, he is called the "father of lies". He is the source from which all lies, deception, temptation and accusation originate. His lies, deception, and accusations are snares that lead us into condemnation (I Tim. 3:6-7 KJV).

Now I want you to stop and consider where all of these "snares of the devil" operate. There is only one place where you believe lies. There is only one place where you can be deceived. There is only one place where you can be tempted. And there is only one place where accusations occur. That place is in your mind in the form of thoughts!

Have you ever experienced the devil appearing in physical form to tempt, deceive, accuse, or condemn you? No - - it always occurs in your thought life. When Jesus was tempted of the devil, I am positive that a character with horns and a pitchfork did not appear to him and tempt him to turn stones into bread.

No - - Jesus had been fasting and was hungry, and the thought came to him that he had the power to do just that. But Jesus recognized the source of that thought and rebuked it.

Here's what I want you to grasp. The battleground is in your human mind - - your thoughts. The soul, which is the invisible realm of thought, will, and emotions, struggles with the spirit, and so, the battle takes place in the realm of thought.

There are many Christians who live miserable lives because they do not understand the strategies of the enemy. They are captured in the snare of the devil and taken captive easily at his will (II Tim. 2:26).

What is the "snare of the devil" that is spoken of here? It is revealed in the previous verse: They oppose themselves. They reject the truth of who they really are and believe that they are the false egoic self created by their own thoughts. They are caught in the snare of a lie. So, they oppose themselves. The flesh (soulish ego) is at war with the spirit.

"For though we live in the world, we do not wage war as the world does. The weapons we fight with are not the weapons of the world. On the contrary, they have divine power to demolish strongholds. We demolish arguments and every pretension that sets itself up against the knowledge of God, and we take captive every thought to make it obedient to Christ." (2 Cor 10:3-5 NIV)

Jesus said that we are in this world but not of it. We are spirit beings living in a material world, but we are not of this material world.

Here Paul writes that we do not wage war as the world does. It also says that the weapons we fight with are not of this world. The KJV says, *"the weapons of our warfare are not carnal"*.

However, the weapons we have are divinely empowered to demolish strongholds. Where are these strongholds located and how do you demolish them?

The strongholds, according to these verses, are your thoughts. You take captive every thought. You demolish arguments and pretensions that come against the knowledge of God.

How do you demolish these strongholds in your mind? We have already seen the answer in Isaiah, *"In repentance and rest is your salvation, in quietness and trust is your strength, but you would have none of it"*.

Your strength comes from quietness and trust. Your salvation from the strongholds in your mind come through repentance, or turning away from the flood of thoughts, and letting your mind rest.

Don't complicate this into some complex religious formula. Obey the simple Word of God that tells us that:

#1 The strongholds are found in your human thoughts.

#2 Your salvation from these strongholds is in turning away, or detaching from those thoughts and letting your mind rest.

#3 Your strength comes from quietness and trust. After giving us the simple solution, God says, "But you would not"!

Too often we think that we should pray more, or fast a few days, or saturate our mind with scripture verses. But how many times have you done this and not come to the abiding peace and unspeakable joy promised by God?

There is a purpose in reading scripture. There is a purpose to prayer and fasting. But there is equally a purpose to learning how to detach from thought and enter the stillness of the Kingdom within.

In my own life, I have found these principals to work time and time again. I can feel turmoil in my soul, and I immediately know that I need to withdraw from my thoughts into my spirit. By doing this, I become detached from the flood of white noise in my mind that feed reactions in my body.

My pulse slows down, my adrenaline system recedes, and I experience a calmness that allows me to respond, instead of react, to the crisis at hand. But this practice is not just intended as a solution to crisis moments.

When we exercise this spiritual principal, we learn to abide permanently in the vine. The secret place of the Most High becomes our constant habitation. We are able to eat in the presence of our enemies (Psalm 23) and not get ulcers.

Paul told us that those who are mature, are those who *"by reason of use have their senses exercised to discern both good and evil"*.

70

By practicing the principal of stillness and quietness we "learn to discern" the soulish from the spiritual. We are able to separate the good from the evil.

Jesus himself practiced withdrawing from thought and entering stillness. He would often get away from the crowds and go to a mountain or the desert where he would escape the noise and activity. He "came apart" before he came apart!

Shortly before his crucifixion, Jesus told his disciples, *"Hereafter, I will not talk much with you: for the prince of this world cometh, and hath nothing in me"* {John 14:30 KJV). Jesus had walked in obedience to the Father and there were no strongholds in him for the enemy to take advantage of. He was tempted in every way that you are, but refused to give in to soulish, egotistic, selfish desires.

But he knew that the ultimate test was coming for him, so he warned his disciples that he would not talk much with them. Isn't that interesting?

He realized his need for quieting his own mind and thoughts and he understood that engaging in too much conversation would hinder his resolve to obey the Father. He was about to enter into the ultimate struggle between his will (soul) and the Father's will (spirit).

Jesus also knew that the enemy would throw everything at him and so he made sure that there was nothing in him that the enemy could build a stronghold around. Remember, that even though he was sinless, he learned obedience through the things he suffered (Hebrews 5:8).

The goal of every Christian is to come to that same place that Jesus was at, where the prince of this world has nothing in you. This is why we must *"let this mind be in you that was in Christ Jesus"* {Philippians 2:5 KJV). We must detach from our natural mind and allow the mind of Christ to operate through us.

Constant chatter and a constant flow of thoughts hinder the flow of the spirit through. Sometimes, like Jesus, we need to talk less and withdraw from the yapping of our thoughts, entering the stillness of our spirit.

Too often the devil is blamed, when in reality, the enemy is our own thoughts. Perhaps the realm of human thinking *is* the devil! It most certainly is the whole realm of his domain as the prince and power of the air (Ephesians 2:2) .

Paul said in II Timothy 25-26 to instruct those who oppose themselves and are taken captive by the snare of the devil at his will.

POGO'S WISDOM
darrell scott

Pogo told us long ago
A truth that sets us free
For he unveiled a secret
That is sometimes hard to see

He calmly made a statement
Without drama – without fuss
He said, "We've met the enemy
The enemy, is us!

So when you point your finger
When you judge, or criticize
Remember Pogo's wisdom
And you soon will realize

The problem's not in others
Or from anything outside
The enemy is plain to see
Your ego and your pride

So when you choose to put away
Your false identity
And let unfold the YOU inside
You'll find that you are free

You'll break the chains of selfish need
Of pressure, and demanding
And live in realms of joy and peace
That pass all understanding

For those who are too young to remember "Pogo", he was a cute little furry animal created by the cartoonist, Walt Kelly. Pogo was known for his wit and whimsical, philosophical quotes. His most famous quote was: "We have met the enemy, and he is us!"

As long as we blame the devil, our parents, our job, an old injury, or anything outside of ourselves, we will never be at peace. The biggest enemy is our own ego that reacts to any perceived threat to its image.

Jesus spoke of *"a peace that the world cannot give, nor take away"*. When we become still in spirit, and learn to observe our thoughts and actions, we come to realize that they are not us.

Thoughts and actions were meant to be manifestations of spiritual intention, not reactive products of the ego. When we realize that the enemy is always "us" - - not the real "us" but the mind-created "us", we have taken the first step away from reaction to the ability to respond.

As we recognize the ego for what it is - - - only a shadow, we then can respond from substance - - - the I AM that I am. The ego can be defined as Edging God Out – E.G.O.

When I am secure with who I am, I never have to live in fear of circumstances or people. I am free to respond instead of reacting. Observing our thoughts and actions in a judgmental way transforms them from enemies to friends.

Chapter 10
THE GOAL OF YOUR FAITH

The goal of your faith is the salvation of your soul. This is clearly stated in I Peter 1:9 (NIV), *"For you are receiving the goal of your faith, the salvation of your souls"*. But what does that mean?

First of all if you interpret this to mean that the goal is for your soul to someday escape punishment and "go to heaven" you are missing the point. I know many people who are miserable in this life, but who are holding on to the hope that their soul will be saved from some horrible fate after they die.

If that has been your thinking, please pamper me and view this verse through a whole new viewpoint. The salvation of your soul is a process in this life that culminates in freedom. *"It is for freedom that Christ set us free"* (Gal. 5:1 KJV).

An important question - - that you know the answer to, is "Do I live in freedom?" If not, your soul has not been restored. A restored soul is described in Psalm 23 (KJV).

It begins with a promise in the form of a statement: *"The Lord is my Shepherd, I shall not want"*. The soul continually wants something. It is continually looking for answers and fulfillment in the "outer" material world.

Your spirit already has all the answers that your soul is seeking for, but the soul (mind, will, and emotions) is at war with the spirit, wanting to rule our lives. Our souls are "lost" and the Good Shepherd was sent to *"seek and save that which was lost"*.

One of the first things that the Good Shepherd must teach the sheep is to stop going his or her own way and follow the Shepherd. When we *"cease from our own labors"* and *"enter His rest"*, we stop wanting or desiring.

Lao Tzu, a wise Chinese philosopher, wrote, "*Ever desireless, one can see the mystery; ever desiring, one sees only the manifestations. And the mystery itself is the doorway to understanding*".
There is tremendous spiritual truth in that statement. This is where the Shepherd wants to take us - - to a place where we are desireless - - we do not want. This is not the end of our spiritual journey; it is only the beginning.

As long as we are desiring, we are seeking the manifestations of spirit, not the mystery of the spirit, or the mystery of the kingdom. Jesus told the woman at the well that he would give her living water that would cause her to never thirst again.

Those who desire, are the seekers. They have not yet entered the mystery, which according to Lao Tzu, is the beginning of understanding. The mystery is the Source. The manifestations are all expressions of the Source.

When we finally grow weary of pursuing the Source through experiences and things, we let go of the manifestations and rest in the provider of the manifestations. The Lord is my Shepherd, I shall not want! I shall not desire!

The 23rd Psalm is an unfolding of the process that takes us on an inward journey to the Kingdom within. It starts at the place where we have become desireless. We shall not want.

As we cease from our own labors - - as we stop desiring - - he takes us into a 2 step process of restoring our soul. First, he makes us lie down in green pastures. And second, he leads us beside still waters. Then he restores our soul.

First, he *makes us* to lie down in green pastures. He doesn't ask us to lie down - - he makes us. How does he do that? By bringing us to the end of ourselves. For some it may be sickness. For others it may be bankruptcy. For some it is depression or disillusionment. But God uses crisis situations to get our attention and make us lie down!

Too many people blame the devil for things that God has ordained. If you look at the book of Job, it was God who initiated all of Job's problems. He asked Satan if he had considered his servant Job and Satan replied that he had, but that God had put a hedge of protection around him. So, God tells Satan that he will tear the hedge down, and basically sics him on the poor man.

Every negative experience Job had was a part of God's plan to bring him to the end of himself and separate the soulish in Job from the spiritual. This becomes clear at the end of the book when Job's family recognizes *"all the evil that the Lord had brought upon him"* (Job 42:11 KJV).

We saw earlier that God lures us into the desert to speak tenderly to us by turning the Valley of Achor (trouble) into a door of hope.

As we are forced to lie down, we begin to realize that he has placed us in green pastures, not parched land. It requires a letting go on our part. It is a picture of entering into his rest and ceasing from our own labors.

There he feeds us with the daily bread, a proceeding, living word; not the stale crusts of doctrines and dogmas of the letter of the word. We feed in a posture of rest.

Secondly, he leads us beside still waters - - not troubled waters. This is a beautiful picture of the spiritual walk. It is in rest, quietness, and trust that he strengthens us.
Be still and know that I am God!

David wrote, *"Be still before the Lord and wait patiently for him; do not fret when men succeed in their ways, when they carry out their wicked schemes - - But the meek shall inherit the land and enjoy great peace"* (Psalm 37:7-11 NIV).

As our soul is being restored, we will continue to experience the storms of life, but if we have followed the Shepherd we will hear his whisper in the wind, *"Peace, be still"*.

The next part of Psalm 23 is interesting: *"He leadeth me in the paths of righteousness for his name's sake"* (KJV). The word *"leadeth"* used here is a Hebrew word, *"nachah"*. This is the only place in the Old Testament where this exact word is used. It is not the same Hebrew word that is used in verse 2, *"He leadeth me beside the still waters"*.

The "leadeth" in verse 2 is a gentle guiding. The "leadeth" in verse 3 is a dragging down paths that you may not want to go down. God will drag you through situations *"for his name's sake"*, to teach you lessons you would never learn unless you go down that particular path. My dear friend, Bob Mumford used to say, "God will hurt you, but he will never harm you!" I have found that statement to be very true.

If you have children, you have drug them into situations for their own good that they would never have chosen to go through on their own. For example, children hate getting a shot at the doctor's office. They hate going to the dentist. But parents understand that sometimes these trips are necessary for the health of their child. The child may go kicking and screaming, but the process is for their good.

God has invested Himself in us and He takes us places we would not choose to go "for His name's sake". This is a part of our journey where we learn the lesson: "not my will, but thine be done"! We eventually learn that His way is better than ours, even if we don't understand it at the time.

Those who think that everything good is from God and everything bad is from the devil, have not matured enough yet. As our soul is restored, we have quieted our mind and learned to follow the inner voice of the spirit, trusting it, even when we would rather go our own way.

As we lie down in green pastures and walk beside still waters our soul is restored enough so that he can drag us down some paths of righteousness, preparing us to experience peace, joy, and wholeness through any outer circumstances that may come our way.

That is why it is a peace that the world cannot give. The world cannot offer a peace that remains when all hell breaks loose in our lives. The world's version of peace is for everything on the outside to be perfect. Perfect marriage, perfect children, perfect job, perfect friends, etc.

But even if we attained all of that, it is a peace based on outward circumstances. The peace of the Kingdom is an abiding peace that passes understanding, because to most people it makes no sense. You can be at peace when everything around you is falling apart. You can be at peace in a traffic jam.

You can be at peace when the stock market crashes. You can be at peace when you lose your job. That is true peace, and it comes from within, not from without.

So, once our soul is restored, and our mind renewed we can experience the next part of Psalm 23: "*Yea, though I walk through the valley of the shadow of death, I will fear no evil - -*". The valley of the shadow of death is the worst possible experience you can ever encounter. But, with a restored soul, there is no fear.

Fear certainly bombards the soul, but the separation of soul and spirit has taken place and you are walking, not in the soulish realm, but in the spirit where there is no fear - - only wholeness, peace, and joy.

You are fully aware of God's abiding presence no matter what you go through. "*For thou art with me*". You realize your oneness with God, the Source of all. This is a fulfillment of the prayer of Jesus when he prayed, "- - *that they may be one, even as we are one; I in them, and thou in me, that they may be made perfect in one - -*" (John 17:22-23 KJV).

This oneness has always been there in your spirit, but it requires a spiritual awakening, followed by a detachment or separation of spirit from soul. Then it is followed by a restoring of the soul and renewing of the mind, that causes you to abide in the "knowing" of who you are.

Moving on in the process of Psalm 23: *"thy rod and thy staff, they comfort me"*. The shepherd's rod was used for defense and discipline, while the staff was used for guidance. When a wolf or other wild animal came to attack the sheep, the shepherd would use the rod to protect the flock. It was an instrument of defense, and the sheep were comforted by the knowledge that the shepherd would protect them.

The second function of the rod was to discipline the sheep. The immature see discipline as a negative thing – something to be avoided, but the restored soul is comforted by the rod of discipline.

"My son, do not make light of the Lord's discipline - - because the Lord disciplines those he loves - - God disciplines us for our good that we may share in his holiness. No discipline seems pleasant at the time, but painful. Later on, however, it produces a harvest of righteousness and peace for those who have been trained by it" (Heb. 12:5-11 NIV).

The spirit understands that the soul will be disciplined by the rod, but is comforted by the fact that it is for the good, and that the end result is alignment (righteousness) and peace.

The shepherd's staff was used for guidance. *"Shepherd your people with your staff, the flock of your inheritance, who dwell alone in a forest in the midst of a garden land"* (Micah 7:14 NIV). The primary functions of the rod were for defense against those that would attack the sheep and discipline for the sheep. However, the primary functions of the staff were for guidance and rescue.

The staff had a crook in the end that would fit snugly around the neck of the sheep. The staff is the trademark of a shepherd.

It is only used by shepherds. It is not used by goat herders, or cattlemen, or by any other profession. And it is only used for sheep.

If a sheep wandered away from the flock and got stranded on a ledge, or fell down a ravine, the shepherd would use the crook in the staff to reach down and help the sheep get back on the path. So, the rod and the staff are both a comfort to the restored soul.

"Thou preparest a table before me in the presence of mine enemies". Wow! An awakened spirit and a restored soul can eat at a table surrounded by enemies and not get ulcers. At this point we have entered the Kingdom fully.

We have peace and joy that is beyond logic. We can walk through the valley of the shadow with no fear and eat in the presence of our enemies with joy.

"Thou anointest my head with oil". The first time "anointing with oil" occurs in the Bible is when Jacob anointed a stone pillar with oil and named it Bethel. Bethel means, "the house of God".

In Psalm 23, as the soul is restored, we receive the approval of God's anointing as we become "Bethel", the house of God. We are the dwelling place, or temple, of God. The Kingdom of God is within us. But the process found Psalm 23 is necessary to reveal to us who we really are. The anointing begins with the head, the place of our thoughts.

This is an image of a renewed mind. God's blessing poured over our head, so that our thoughts are gone and his thoughts now flow. We no longer have a carnal, or fleshly mind. We have the mind of Christ.

"My cup runneth over". The process of detachment from thought is complete. The separation of soul and spirit has occurred. The indwelling wholeness, peace, and joy are a permanent abode. Our spirit and soul are in alignment with the Source. Now, we are blessed beyond our ability to contain it.

80

So we begin to pour out, or overflow onto others. The ultimate calling is to serve others from a heart of love.

"May the Lord make your love increase and overflow for each other and for everyone else, just as ours does for you" (1 Thess 3:12 NIV)

"Surely goodness and mercy shall follow me all the days of my life". Notice that they follow you. You have to turn around and look back to see them. When they were beside you they felt like trouble and suffering, but the process of restoring your soul transforms them into goodness and mercy.

How often have you looked back on an experience of sorrow or loss, and been able to say, "I am so thankful that I went through that"? It is not something you would have chosen to go through, but something that you were dragged through "for his name's sake" for your good.

The last phrase of Psalm 23 is proof that the transformation has taken place. *"And I will dwell in the house of the Lord forever"*. Awareness has come through spiritual awakening, separation of soul and spirit, and renewing of the mind.

"I am one with the Father - - with the Source of all things." The storms may come and go, but your house is built on the rock. You know who you are and why you are here. You have now found the "secret place of the Most High" and will abide there forever. You have received the goal of your faith: the salvation of your soul!

Chapter 11
LET "I AM" SAY "YES" TO THE "NOW"

All of our problems: disgruntlement, complaining, and frustration originate from not accepting what life has put in front of us at this moment. We want it to be different; we want to change it; we refuse to accept it. Say our ego says, 'No!' to what is.

"Always say 'yes' to the present moment - - Surrender to what is. Say 'yes' to life and see how life suddenly starts working for you rather than against you."   Eckhart Tolle

 Have you ever tried to change someone like your spouse, or partner, or child, or parent? How well did that go? Have you ever thought, "If he or she would just change in this or that area my life would be so much happier"?

Only when the real me, the I AM, comes into alignment with what is, will we experience peace. Saying 'yes' to the moment does not necessarily mean that we like it or that we can't and shouldn't do something about it. It means that we stop fighting it, accept it, and then out of peace do what needs to be done.

The truth is, when we stop trying to change people and we embrace them just the way they are, they seem to change! Wayne Dyer said, "When you change the way you look at things, the things you look at change".

All we ever have is now! Past is gone and lives in memory only. Present awareness cannot exist while we are reminiscing about the past or planning for the future. Future only exists in imagination, either with anxiety or anticipation. But all we have and will ever have is NOW.

Memory and planning both have their place, but too often they are the source of the "white noise" in our head that blocks out the peace, joy, and wholeness of the spiritual life. Sometimes thoughts of the past replay themselves over and over in your mind creating tension in your body from thoughts about what you coulda, shoulda, or woulda done if you could go back and do it over again.

When we make peace with now, our inner being is aware. We stop living in the past or future. We observe our thoughts and actions and align them with our spirit instead of letting them control us. The following poem came to me as I sat in peace, simply being aware:

When "I AM" Says "Yes" to the NOW
darrell scott

I once tried to change, the things I distained
Frustrated – I didn't know how
Then deep from within, this truth did ascend
"Let 'I AM' say 'YES' to the NOW"

It took me a while, but soon with a smile
My innermost being did bow
Away from my mind, where soon I would find
That 'I AM' says 'YES' to the 'NOW'

I've learned to let go – to merge with the flow
No longer by sweat of my brow
My struggles all cease, and I enter peace
When 'I AM' says 'YES' to the NOW

So clearly I see, my thoughts are not me
To "being" I offer my vow
My life is not planned by ego's demand
When 'I AM' says 'YES' to the 'NOW'

All wars will dissolve, and peace will evolve
Such beauty the Source will allow
Deep love we will see, and great harmony
When 'I AM' says 'YES' to the NOW

Embrace life each moment and you will experience life each moment. Simply learn to say "Yes" to whatever the present moment brings.

The following quotations are from men and women who have learned to detach from thought, and live in the present moment. Their words of universal wisdom apply to anyone in any situation of life.

"Take therefore not thought for the morrow; for the morrow shall take thought for the things of itself". Jesus

"Happiness, not in another place, but this place - - not for another hour, but this hour" Walt Whitman

"The present moment is filled with joy and happiness. If you are attentive, you will see it - - - Live the actual moment. Only this moment is life" Thich Nhat Hahn

"The secret of health for both mind and body is not to mourn for the past, or to anticipate troubles, but to live in the present moment wisely and earnestly" Buddha

Here is another poem I wrote concerning the robbers of past and future:

ROBBERS
darrell scott

Past and future - - thieves that steal
What the present would reveal
Lost in memories, dreams, and goals
While ignoring what is real

Backward look and forward glance
Keep us bound within a trance
Stealing chapters of our lives
Unaware of present chance

Peace and joy are never found
When our search is outward bound
Both await from deep within
While we're seeking all around

Trading now for what will be
Or some bygone memory
Unaware of here and now
Blinded from reality

Spirit speaks through quieted mind
Oh what treasures there we'll find
When the stillness grips our soul
Peace and joy and love divine

The title of a famous Beatles song encompasses the truth expressed in the poem. "Let It Be". Paul McCartney wrote this song when he was going through a rough time in his life. When he was 14 years old, his mother died, but years later, as an already famous member of the Beatles he had a dream. In the dream, his mother, Mary gave him some good advice. Here's how Paul described it:

"So in this dream twelve years later, my mother appeared, and there was her face, completely clear, particularly her eyes, and she said to me very gently, very reassuringly: "Let it be."

It was lovely. I woke up with a great feeling. It was really like she had visited me at this very difficult point in my life and gave me this message: Be gentle, don't fight things, just try and go with the flow and it will all work out.

So, being a musician, I went right over to the piano and started writing a song: "When I find myself in times of trouble, Mother Mary comes to me"... Mary was my mother's name... "Speaking words of wisdom, let it be."

While my poem, *"When "I AM" says "YES" to the NOW"* will never be as well known as McCartney's song, *"Let It Be"*, the message is the same. Learn to flow with what life presents at the present moment instead of always wanting to change it.

A children's song that was written in the 1850's gives us a blueprint for successful living. The song, which we all know, goes: *"Row, row, row, your boat gently down the stream. Merrily, merrily, merrily, merrily, life is but a dream"*.

The first lesson found in the poem is to row, row, row - - . It is interesting that it repeats the instruction 3 times. This describes the first steps that lead us to living merrily, merrily, merrily, merrily! Three "rows" that lead to four "merrily's". "Row" indicates work.

This corresponds with the scriptures in Hebrews that say, "Strive to enter in to rest". Rowing is the seeking stage that precedes the finding and releasing stages. It requires effort to teach us that effort is not the best way. The lesson we learn from rowing is followed by "gently" and "down the stream".

The second lesson from this song is to row *your* boat - - not everybody else's! If you want to live a life of misery, just attempt to row other people's boats for them. Have you ever been successful at trying to row someone else's boat? I seriously doubt it.

The closer we are in relationship to someone, the more tempted we are to row each other's boat. But each boat is designed uniquely for its' own occupant. You know the frustration you feel when someone else attempts to row your boat, so refrain from trying to row theirs!

The third lesson is to row your boat *gently*. Get into the rhythm of life and be aware of the present moment. Learn to go with the flow. Gentleness is not to be mistaken for weakness. As Paul's mother, Mary, said in the dream, "Let it be". This applies to the past and the future as well.

Sometimes your boat bumps around in turbulent waters because of past memories in which you were wronged by others, or in some cases, where you've wronged others. Sometimes it hits the raging currents of disappointments over future dreams that never are fulfilled.

And last, but not least, row your boat gently *down the stream.* Let the past 'be'. Allow the future to 'be'. And most importantly, learn to 'be' in the moment! Say "Yes" to the "Now" and you can merrily, merrily, merrily, merrily enjoy life as though it were a dream.

In the last chapter we saw that the goal of our faith is the salvation of our soul. We have looked at the process through the Biblical lenses of Psalm 23, but the realization of that goal is always available. It is today - - it is now. " - - *now is the accepted time, behold, now is the day of salvation*" (II Cor. 6:2 KJV).

The moment you choose to let go of your own thoughts and ways, you can turn to the still waters within and find rest for your soul (see Matt. 11:29 KJV). Jesus said, "*Come unto me all ye that labor and are heavy laden and I will give you rest*". He did not say that you must earn it, he said that he would give it to you. Where do we go to in order to access this "rest"? It is within us.

Chapter 12
OFF WITH THEIR HEADS

The Queen of Hearts in the classic story of "Alice in Wonderland" was often heard screaming *"Off with their heads!"*. Perhaps there is a much deeper meaning in, not only the statement she made, but in who she was.

She was the Queen of Hearts, not the Queen of Minds. The heart and the head are often in disagreement. Sometimes the head would like to rip out the heart while the heart often desires a beheading to take place.

In scripture, the soul seems to be aligned with the head, while the spirit seems to be in alignment with the heart. I give much credit to my dear friend, Dr. Mark Hanby, for his insight concerning much of the content in this chapter.

In the book of Revelation, John *"saw the souls of those who had been beheaded because of the testimony of Jesus and because of the word of God"* (Revelation 20:4 NAS). Notice that it says the souls, not spirits, of those who had been beheaded.

Also notice that it was " - - *because of the word of God"*. They were not allowed to enter into the Holy of Holies, the secret place of the Most High, the place of rest, until they lost their heads. Perhaps it was the sword of the spirit, the word of God that beheaded them!

I know that many will read this and believe that it is talking about physical beheading, but what if it is something deeper than that. Could it be that the King of Hearts has declared that the entrance to the inner chambers can only be attained by the word of God severing soul and spirit, causing "Off with their heads" to be a legitimate qualification for entering the "rest" God spoke of in Hebrews?

Now look further at a connecting passage in Revelation 6:9-11, "- - - *I saw underneath the altar the souls of those who had been slain*

88

because of the word of God - - - and they were told that they should rest for a little while longer, until the number of their - - brethren who were to be killed even as they had been, should be completed also".

I purposely left out portions of these verses to emphasize some important things that I think we should consider. These 2 sets of verses from Revelation chapters 6 and 20 are clearly referring to the same people. These people are described in the following manner:

#1 Their souls were underneath the altar, not their spirits

#2 Their souls were slain by being beheaded (off with their heads)

#3 They had been beheaded *because* of the word of God (the Greek word for "because" (*dia*) can also be translated "by")

#4 While their souls were observed being under the altar, they were at rest

#5 They were waiting for their friends (brethren) to be beheaded, just like they had been

The book of Revelation is full of symbolism and metaphorical statements that reveal pictures, not to be taken literally, but to point toward a deeper truth. For example, Jesus is described as having hair white as wool (symbolic of purity), feet of brass (judgment), and a sword hanging out of his mouth (the word of God).

I don't believe that anyone would take that as a literal description of Jesus, i.e. that he was white-headed and clopped around with brass feet while a sword dangled from his mouth, cutting his lips every time he talked.

So if we seek the deeper truth from the above scriptures, perhaps it would reveal to us that we are not allowed to enter into the "secret place of the Most High" until we have been beheaded - - or left our minds and thoughts at the altar.

In that verse where it says, *"because of the word of God"*, the word *"because"* is *"dia"* in Greek and, according to Strong's Concordance, it is often translated *"by"*.

For example in Matthew 2:5 it reads, " - - *it is written by (dia) the prophet"*. In that verse it was the prophet who did the writing, it was not written because of the prophet, but by the prophet.

If we read that John *"saw the souls of those who had been beheaded - - **by** (dia) the word of God"* and compare that with the sword of God that severs soul and spirit in Hebrews 4:12 it makes perfect sense.

It is the souls that were to be left at the altar, not the spirits. The spirits are allowed to enter the Holy of Holies where they are at rest, waiting for others to lose their heads and join them.

In Hebrews it talks about a "rest" that God has called us to. I mentioned this in previous chapters, but would like to examine it more closely:

"For the one who has entered into His rest has himself also rested from his works, as God did from His. Let us therefore be diligent to enter that rest, lest anyone fall through following the same example of disobedience"(Hebrews 4:10-11 NAS).

As we have seen already, we are called to enter into "rest". Jesus said, *"Come to me, all that are weary and heavy-laden, and I will give you rest. Take my yoke upon you and learn from me, for I am gentle and humble in heart, and you will find rest for your souls"* (Matthew 11:28-29 NAS). Notice that he said *"rest for your souls"*, not your spirits!

So when you put all this together, you see that when we come unto Jesus we will find rest for our souls (our "psychais"). It is the mind, the psyche, that needs rest. It is the psyche (soul) that is found under the altar after a beheading. It is the beheaded psyche that is allows our spirit (pnuema) to enter into rest.

So how do we enter into the rest? By the sword of the living word of God severing the domination of our thinking mind. That is clearly seen in the verse that follows Hebrews 4:10-11 which talks about entering into God's rest and ceasing from our own labors.

The very next verse (12) says, *"For (*or because) *the word of God Living and active and sharper than any two-edged sword, and piercing as far as the division of soul and spirit - - "*.

BEHEAD US, O GOD
darrell scott

May the sword of God behead us,
As we follow in His quest
Separating soul and spirit
So we enter into rest

Tearing down the mighty strongholds
Of our thoughts and in our mind
Bringing peace through true alignment
And abundant joy divine

Another thing that I want to look at concerning entering God's rest can be found in Hebrew 3:9-11 (NAS): *"Where your fathers tried me by testing me, and saw my works for forty years. Therefore I was angry with this generation, and said, 'They always go astray in their hearts; and the did not know my ways'. As I swore in my wrath, 'They shall not enter my rest'.* This is a quote from Psalm 91 which also talks about God's works versus His ways.

The children of Israel wandered around in the wilderness for forty years where they saw miracle after miracle occur. They watched the Red Sea part, allowing them to walk across on dry ground. They watched as Pharaoh's army drowned when the walls of water came back together behind them.

They saw the rock in the desert as it split and water gushed out to provide them with refreshing drink.

They saw the manna fall from heaven, the pillar of fire, and many other miracles. They witnessed the works of God over and over again, but they never came to understand His ways!

How frustrated Moses must have been to work with this huge crowd of people who received from, but never understood the Source that provided for them.

"He made known His ways to Moses, His deeds to the people of Israel" (Psalm 103:7 NIV). The reason they never experienced the "rest" that God provided, was because they only saw his works, or deeds. They never reached the maturity of Moses, who understood His ways.

There are multitudes of believers who, in this lifetime, will never enter into the "rest" that God has made available to them now. They are not willing to leave their heads at the altar. Unwilling to allow the sword of God to sever their soul and spirit. Unwilling to learn how to be still and know. And yet, as Hebrews says, there remains a rest, waiting for them to enter into.

All of this corresponds to what Jesus said: *"Whoever finds their live (pysche) will lose it, and whoever loses their life (pysche), for my sake, will find it"* (Matthew 10:39 NIV). The Greek word for "life" is actually "zoe", but it is not used in this verse.

Instead the word normally translated soul is used here, pysche. Psyche is where we get the word psychology, which is the study of the mind, or soul. So Jesus was saying, "If you want to find your mind, you've got to lose your mind"!

The freedom that we find when we let go of our thoughts is worth the cost. My daughter, Rachel, loved a quote by Jim Elliot, who said, *"He is no fool who gives what he cannot keep, to gain what he cannot lose"*. Jim and 4 of his friends were speared to death by natives in Ecuador that they were trying to minister too.

Later Jim's wife traveled back through the jungle to help the very people who had murdered her husband. My son, Craig, was involved in the movie about Jim and his friends, and even played a small role, acting as Jim, in the movie.

The renewing of the mind is a Biblical concept that is often lightly addressed, or even ignored. But it is essential to not only understand the need for a renewed mind, but to understand how that is obtained.

Perhaps it is the removal, instead of the renewal that we should consider. God said that his thoughts and ways are not ours. We are told that the natural mind is an enemy of God. We are told that we need the mind of Christ. All of this lends itself to a beheading of the soulish mind and a replacement of the spiritual mind.

When Adam and Eve ate from the Tree of the Knowledge of Good and Evil, and their minds were corrupted (II Cor. 11:3), they were cast out of the Garden of Eden to prevent them from eating from the Tree of Life. An angel with a flaming sword was placed at the entrance to the garden to prevent them from going back in.

We are promised that in Christ we can eat of the Tree of Life, we can return back to the Garden, but we have to be beheaded to get back in. You can't go in with a natural mind that is full of the fruit of the Knowledge of Good and Evil.

Chapter 13
THE PHILIPPIANS FORMULA

The book of Philippians provides a release from the prison of your thoughts that allows you to enter the lasting peace that abides in your spirit. For most people, peace is a rare commodity, and joy is just as scarce.

The truth is, they are there in abundance, but the "white noise" of our thoughts have locked them up. But there is a secret place where both peace and joy are permanent. It is referred to as "the secret place of the Most High" and, as we have seen, it is within you. For the Kingdom of God is: righteousness, peace, and joy and, as Jesus said, it is within you.

Paul explains that he has learned this secret to lasting peace and contentment. He wrote, "*I have learned to be content whatever the circumstances. I know what it is to be in need, and I know what it is to have plenty. I have learned the secret of being content in any and every situation, whether well fed or hungry, whether living in plenty or in want*" (Philippians 4:11-12 NIV). He calls it a "secret", the secret of contentment!

It is important to note that he is writing this letter while he is in a cold, smelly prison with chains around his ankles. From this miserable condition, he writes about joy and peace. In another place he wrote, "*I pray to God that not only you, but all who are listening to me today, may become what I am, except for these chains*" (Acts 26:29 NIV).

So, how can a person be full of joy and peace and be in such terrible circumstances? Paul says that he has *learned the secret of being content.* In other words, the secret to being content is a learned skill.

There is a thief that comes to steal, kill, and destroy our peace. This thief causes anxiety, depression, worry, discontent, sorrow, and many other distressing symptoms, all in the realm of your soul, your psyche. And he has a secret weapon to do this with.

The weapon is thoughts, or more specifically, attachment to thoughts. There are 3 main channels that the thief uses, and they are circumstances, people, and things.

It is your thoughts that create worry, anxiety, etc., about the circumstances, people, and things in your life. You have met people who worry about everything. You have met people who are reliving memories of the past with regret.

You have met people who are anxious about the future. Perhaps you are one of those. The first step in tapping into the inner peace is to let go of all that worry, stress, and anxiety.

This is why Jesus said, *"Take no **thought** for the morrow"*. The only time you will ever have is NOW. Do not waste it with regret about the past or anxiety about the future. Only when you learn to be still, and know the I AM within you in this present moment will you experience peace. God is not the "I WAS", or the "I WILL BE", He is the "I AM", and He dwells in you.

But what if you could experience peace, instead of anxiety when you lose your job, or your car is stolen, or you lose a friend. This is the secret that Paul writes about. The secret of entering the peace that passes understanding when all hell breaks loose in your life.

The answer centers around your mind and your thoughts. In the small book of Philippians, Paul uses the words "mind", "think", "thought", and "remember" 15 times. He understood that the right alignment of our mind and heart, our soul and spirit, would bring peace, contentment, and joy.

So, let's take a look at the components of the "secret" Paul wrote about. The secret is found by skipping around the book of Philippians and putting the pieces together. Truth and wisdom come from God in this manner: *"For whom shall He teach knowledge, and whom shall He make to understand? - - For precept must be upon precept, line upon line, line upon line. Here a little, and there a little"* (Isaiah 28:9-10 KJV).

This is the secret to finding the secret! It is given to us in pieces. God's ways are not our ways, so he hides truth in pieces, so that we will search for it. *"It is the glory of God to conceal a matter; to search out a matter is the glory of kings"* (Proverbs 25:2 NIV).

I want to start with something important that Paul says to those he is writing too. He says, *"Join in following my example, and observe those who walk according to the pattern you have in us"* (Philippians 3:17 NAS).

It is important to follow people who don't just talk about peace and contentment, but actually live it. So, although you may not know me, I can tell you honestly that the things I am about to write about have led me to a place that Paul wrote about.

Paul had been around the block a few times and he wrote about his experiences and credentials in chapter 3:4-6. He pointed out that if anyone had a reason to boast it would be him. He was circumcised the 8th day, of the tribe of Benjamin, a Hebrew of Hebrews, zealous of the law, trained by the great teacher Gamaliel, blameless, etc. He was qualified to be not only a teacher, but a role model as well.

While not comparing myself with Paul, I also have been around enough to observe and learn a few things. I have walked through the nightmare of losing my daughter, Rachel Joy Scott, in the Columbine high school shooting and come to know the peace of God that passes understanding. I have traveled with my friends, Josh McDowell, Bob Cornuke, and David Barton and spoken in World View conferences at some of the largest churches in America.

I have spoken, several times on TBN, spoken at Liberty University, and was part of initiating "The Call" in Washington, D.C. with Lou Engles and Josh McDowell, where myself, Dr. Bill Bright and many others spoke to 400,000 Christian youth. I have spoken on over 100 campuses doing events for Campus Crusade to packed crowds at Auburn University, Texas A&M, Princeton University, William and Mary, and many more.

I have keynoted for over 50 banquets at Youth for Christ events around the nation. I have sat and met with President Trump at Trump Tower with leaders like Rick Joyner, Frank Amedia, and Sid Roth.

I have been invited to meet with President Clinton in the Oval Office, with President G.W. Bush backstage at a conference, and with President Trump in the Presidential Dining Room at the White House. I have spoken before Congress twice. I have appeared on Oprah, CNN, Today Show, and many others. I have been featured in Time magazine and quoted in Newsweek and the Wall Street Journal. But, like Paul, I have learned to have no confidence in the flesh.

However, I have come to observe that the majority of Christians I have known, including many big names in the Christian community, have never learned how to walk in peace and contentment. I have found some of them to be humble men and women who have discovered the secret, and I have found many that have big egos and ambitions that will never allow them to discover their true self, or enjoy the treasures of the Kingdom within.

Just because a person is a Christian, or even a pastor, or spiritual leader, does not mean that he or she walks in alignment, peace, and joy. Sadly, many of them do not understand what it means to have a renewed mind.

They still operate from the white noise of a carnal mind, instead of from the mind of Christ. They still identify themselves with their thoughts.

With that being said, let me echo the pieces of the secret that Paul gives us in Philippians. The first is to imitate those who have demonstrated the peace and contentment he wrote about.

Now, let's look at another piece of the secret: He writes in Philipians 4:8 (NIV), "*Do not be anxious about anything*". How do you not be anxious?

97

The things I am about to tell you, I have practiced and they work. They may not sound spiritual, but the basis of these practices are found throughout scripture.

Anxiety has numerous expressions including, depression, worry, fear, anger, criticism, etc. It all comes from an undisciplined mind that needs renewing, whether one is a believer or not. In today's culture, drugs have become the answer to dealing with anxiety. Especially prescription drugs.

Believers who would not think of using marijuana or crack, will not hesitate to pop legal prescription drugs to calm their nerves and ease their anxiety.
This is not an attack on those people, nor a condemnation of their practices, but simply an offer to show a better way.

I have learned 7 simple steps that eliminate anxiety and open the door to peace. These 7 steps are summed up in Philippians 2:5-2, and begin with the words, *"Let this mind be in you"* (KJV). The seven steps are as follows:

#1 Who being in the form of God
#2 Thought it not robbery to be equal with God
#3 But made of himself no reputation
#4 He humbled himself
#5 And became obedient
#6 Unto death, even the death of the cross
#7 Wherefore, God has highly exalted him

Notice these 7 steps begin with the instruction to "let this mind be in you". You must know and understand that these 7 steps apply, not only to Jesus, but also to you. I emphasize that because, much of what you have learned through religion will resist some of what I am about to say.

Step #1: WHO BEING IN THE FORM OF GOD. It is extremely important to understand that you and I were made in His image or

form. In the very first chapter of the Bible it tells us that: "*God created man in his own image*" (Genesis 1:27 KJV).
In chapter 5 it says: "*In the day that God created man, in the likeness of God made he him*" (Genesis 5:1 KJV).

You must know that you are created in God's image at the deepest level of your being. That is your true identity. The first step toward fulfilment, peace, and joy is to clearly understand who you are. *Let this mind be in you.*

Step #2: THOUGHT IT NOT ROBBERY TO BE EQUAL WITH GOD. The Greek rendering of this says, "not something to be grasped at". Some translations say he did not use his equality with God for his own advantage. This is the one that religion will have the most difficulty with.

The real you is divine (John 10:34). Your spirit is the candle of the Lord (Proverbs 20:27). The Kingdom of God dwells within you (Luke 17:21 KJV). You are a partaker in the divine nature (II Peter 1:4 NAS). You are the light of the world (Matthew 5:14). Jesus prayed, "that they may be one, even as you and I are one" (John 17:22). We have denied our gift of divinity far too long.

"*I (God), said, "You are gods. You are all sons of the Most High*" (Psalm 82:6 NIV). Jesus quotes from this passage in John 10:34: "*Is it not written in your Law, I have said you are gods*".

This is not an ego trip. This is an acknowledgement of Biblical truth. You, that is your spirit, is a part of the divine. The Greek language says that equality with God was not something Jesus grasped at. We are not to grasp at the divinity within, but we are to acknowledge it. *Let this mind be in you.*

When you know the truth of who you are, all self-condemnation and feelings of unworthiness are eliminated. You live with the confidence that you *are* the righteousness of God in Christ (II Corinthians 5:21).

The first step to freedom is to know the truth about yourself, and the truth will set you free. Too often religion has emphasized the weakness of your flesh instead of the divinity of your spirit.

There is much more that I could say about these first two steps, but it is critically important to understand who you are before you can go to the next step.

Step #3: BUT MADE OF HIMSELF NO REPUTATION. Once we know who we are, we have nothing to prove. In the classic story of Superman, Clark Kent walked around as a mild mannered reporter, but he knew who he really was. The false self, the ego, loves to enhance its reputation.

The ego is created from your attachment to thoughts about yourself. Therefore, it is important to maintain and reinforce those thoughts with approval from others, keeping up appearances, name-dropping, etc. The ego wants to look good, feel good, and be right!
The ego likes attention and will seek it in many forms, including self-pity, and even shyness.

We often think of the bold, outgoing person as having a big ego. The truth is, everyone that is attached to their thoughts about themselves have egos. The ego must die in order for your true self to emerge. We will see that in future steps.

Step #4: HE HUMBLED HIMSELF. The Greek language says, he emptied himself. Once you recognize who you are, you can have the confidence to empty your false self without an identity crisis. This emptying can be painful, because it requires a letting go of all the false impressions and the reputation you have worked hard at creating.

One of the most humbling scenes in the whole Bible is found in John 13, where Jesus washed the feet of his disciples. This was considered the duty of slaves, not the duty of the Master! These men walked all day in dusty, filthy sandals and there feet would be smelly and coated with dirt. The disciples were appalled at what he was doing.

But notice why he had the confidence and humility to do this: "*Jesus knowing that the Father had given all things into his hands, and that he was come from God, and went to God. He riseth from supper, and laid aside his garments, and took a towel and girded himself. After that he poureth water into a basin, and began to wash the disciples' feet*" (John 13:3-5 KJV).

What I want you to focus on, is not that he washed their feet, but what gave him the grace and confidence to do that. It says 3 things: #1 He knew that the Father had given all things unto his hands, #2 He knew that he came from God, and #3 He knew that he was going back to God.

He knew where he came from, what he had, and where he was going! Unfortunately most people, including Christians, don't understand those things about themselves. You must know that "*all things are yours*" (I Corinthians 3:21). You must know that you "*can do all things*" (Philippians 4:13). You must know that He has "*blessed us with all spiritual blessings*" (Ephesians 1:3).
If you know these things, then you are able to let go of reputation and empty your ego. *Let this mind be in you.*

I practice something every morning when I first get up, that I recommend to you. In the shower, I consciously empty myself of the white noise of thoughts and express gratitude for who I am and what I have been given.

Part of that process includes observing my thoughts and realizing that they are not me. In observing them, I have learned to detach completely from my thoughts and enter the stillness of the spirit. With practice this becomes easier and easier. Paul said that we exercise our spiritual senses by reason of use (Hebrews 5:14).

The practice in the shower has now become a part of my life throughout each day.

At red lights, in meetings, in my office, and outdoors, I have learned to detach from thought by emptying myself, my ego, and being grateful for who I am.

What are we "emptying ourselves" of? What are we destroying from our mind in the "stillness"? *"We are destroying speculations and every lofty thing raised up against the knowledge of God - - "* (II Corinthians 10:5 NAS).

The treasure hidden within your spirit is opposed by the enemy in your mind - - which is your thoughts. What are these speculations and lofty things raised up against the knowledge of God? They are thoughts, the white noise of an untamed mind.

What keeps us from the knowledge of God? It is the movement of thought. *"Be still and know that I am God"* (Psalm 46:10). *"In repentance and rest is your salvation, in quiet and trust is your strength, but you would have none of it"* (Isaiah 30:15 NIV). We must not do as Israel who were unwilling and disobedient.

Step #5: AND BECAME OBEDIENT. The only reason it took the children of Israel 40 years to go from Egypt to Canaan was because they were not obedient. Their refused to believe what God had told them about themselves and what he had already given them. He said, *"If you are willing and obedient, you will eat the good of the land"* (Isaiah 1:19 NIV). A trip that should have taken them 40 days, instead, took them 40 years, because they were not willing and obedient.

A lot of Christians are sacrificing their time, their money, and their lives in an effort to obtain the peace, joy, and fulfillment God has promised. I have met many well-intended people who have failed because they thought they could reach the goal through self effort. But *"to obey is better than to sacrifice"* (I Samuel 15:22).

Obedience to the still small voice cannot happen until we can actually hear the still small voice. The voice speaks from our spirit, not our mind.

102

It is our mind that is constantly creating noise in the form of thoughts. Our salvation comes through a turning away from that noise, or repentance from that noise. Only then can we enter the rest, the quiet, and the trust which we saw in Isaiah 30:15.

The only way true obedience can happen is when we pray, as Jesus prayed, *"Not my will, but thine be done"*. The mind, the thoughts, and the will, are all a part of the soul, the psyche. It is the spirit that we must learn to hear and obey. *Let this mind be in you.*

Step #6 UNTO DEATH, EVEN THE DEATH OF THE CROSS. This step is impossible without having practiced the first 5 steps. This applies to you, not just to Jesus. Jesus told us that *"Whoever wants to be my disciple must deny themselves and take up their cross and follow me"* (Mark 8:34 NIV).

The description of what is being asked for here is brutal, but necessary. If you understand the divinity within you, have emptied your false self, and have become obedient, the next step is to deny that false self and allow it to be completely crucified.

You see it for what it is: an egoic imposter that has kept you imprisoned by thoughts and speculations resulting in condemnation, judgment, criticism, depression, and anxiety. *"We take captive every thought to make it obedient to Christ"* (II Corinthians 10:5 NIV).

You are now abiding in your position (In Christ) and your condition has become, Christ in you. You are walking in the spirit, not the flesh. The straight and narrow way that leads to life can only be entered through the cross. *Let this mind be in you.*

Step #7 WHEREFORE, GOD HAS HIGHLY EXALTED HIM. This is the goal! That we become exalted, not in ego, but in spirit. That we eat the good of the land. That we experience the alignment, peace and joy, promised to us! Humble yourself in the sight of the Lord and He will lift you up!

You were meant to be the light of world. You are the candle of the Lord. You are the righteousness of God. You are the salt of the earth. You are the only Jesus that the world can see! If these words are not heard in light of the first 6 steps they sound heretical. But they are scriptural, spiritual truths that we were called to experience and "be"!

He wants to trust us enough to put us before kings and rulers. He intended for us to influence the world around us, not hide behind four walls on Sunday morning. But there are no shortcuts. To have the mind of Christ requires all of the steps I have talked about. My dear friend, Bob Mumford, and I have discussed these steps at length, and I give him much credit to the content of this chapter.

Chapter 14
THE WATCHER

A newborn infant is fully aware. It has not yet become a thinker. Once cognitive skills are developed, the child slowly loses its awareness identity and becomes so occupied with thought that it begins to believe it is the thoughts themselves. Nothing could be further from the truth. This is where the ego, the false self, emerges. Attachment to, and identity with, thought.

Many poets and philosophers have written that we have forgotten who we are. You must embark on a journey back to awareness before you can ever find fulfillment. Socrates gave us his greatest words of wisdom when he simply said, "Know thyself".

To know one's ego is not to know one's true self. Ego is a false self, created by the thinking mind. It is a creation of the soul, not the spirit. It is created and projected from your thoughts and the thoughts and opinions of others around you. The false self is a composition of your history and story in this physical world. Your true identity, your spirit, goes much deeper than your story and your history.

As long as your false self is dominant, you live in frustration. There may be an appearance of happiness on the surface, but beneath that appearance is an uneasy dissatisfaction. The ego can never bring fulfillment.

As you practice observing your thoughts and actions, you come to realize that they are not you. Your salvation from the prison of false selfhood comes through quiet and stillness. The quieting of the mind allows stillness. The stillness allows detachment from thought. Detachment from thought dissolves the ego, or false self, allowing the I AM that is you to ascend into freedom.

Awareness that you are speaking or acting from your ego instead of from your true self, immediately gets you out of the ego. The moment you begin to observe your ego, you are no longer acting from it. The ego craves attention and will prompt you to do, and say things, that are out of character with who you really are.

Think of the ego as the surface of an ocean and the real self as the stillness down below the surface. The surface is constantly changing and moving by the influence of the weather, the moon, or other external factors. However, the depth of the ocean remains peaceful and calm regardless of what is happening on the surface.

Too many remain at the surface level of their lives reacting to everything that happens to them. Choose to go deeper, and you will discover your true self.

One of the first steps to dissolving the ego is to become a watcher, or observer, of the myriad of thoughts that continually are going through your mind. If you take a moment, close your eyes, and try to watch the thoughts that go through your head, you will be amazed at how fast they come and go. There is so much chatter going on all the time that we are hardly even aware of.

As you first begin to observe your thoughts, you will find that it is difficult to focus because they come and go so fast. The minute you begin "thinking about a thought" instead of just observing it, you have lost the role of "watcher" and have slipped back into the role of "thinker".

With practice, you will begin to feel detached from the thoughts that are zipping through your mind. You will probably notice that all of your thoughts are either taking you into the past by way of memory, or projecting you into the future with plans, appointments, etc.

In the practice of Zen there is what is called the "thinking mind" and the "observing mind". The thinking mind is what rules most of humanity. I refer to the observing mind as spirit (pneuma) and the thinking mind as soul (psyche).

Most people have absolutely no control over their thought life. It requires intentionality to develop the "observing mind" that can eventually allow us to detach from the "thinking mind" at will.

But unless we take the time to develop the "observing mind", the "thinking mind" will capture us at its will. It is our attachment to thoughts that lead us into negative emotions and harmful actions.

If you have a partner or spouse, most likely you have predictable heated arguments. It starts off with some harmless conversation about something that happened a year ago and she or she says, "No, it was two years ago" and the argument begins.

The ego sparks up through the thinking mind and wants to be right. So the thoughts become more and more agitated and migrate into emotions. These emotions begin to accelerate and spill over into actions that you may regret.

The thing that sparked the argument is different each time, but the pattern is predictable. We become the slaves to our own soulish ego and its reactions.

If in the beginning of the argument, you can practice using your observing mind, there is a possibility of defusing the situation before it becomes uncontrollable.

You can observe your initial emotional reaction to your partner and through observation actually detach from the thinking that prompted the emotion. This cuts off the fuel for the emotional reaction and it dies.

Next time you are engaging in a disagreement with another person, observe your own thoughts, feelings, and actions. You will eventually be able to respond instead of always reacting.

It is important to not try and stop the thoughts or feelings, but to simply observe them.

The observation quickly takes away the compulsion and you can experience peace in the situation that you normally would be uptight and tense, or even angry in.

It is possible to experience anxiety in your soul (psyche) and at the same time feel deep peace in your spirit (pnuema). When this dichotomy happens, do not engage the anxiety. Acknowledge it and let go of it.

You might send a message from your place of observing to the anxiety that says, "I acknowledge that I feel anxiety, but that is not who I am." You are the observer not the anxiety.

Remember that the more you resist a negative thought or feeling, the more you empower it. The more you resist, the more they persist. You may replace thoughts of resistance with awareness: "I am not depressed, I just feel depressed". "My wife (or husband) is not mean, it just feels like she (or he) is mean right now".

Remember the real you is the I AM. Do not add negative descriptions to who you are. I AM angry. I AM stupid. I AM hungry. None of these are you. They are what your thoughts through your body, cause you to feel at times.

And finally, I have found that if I can practice being thankful for everything that happens to me, the gratitude transforms even the worst experiences eventually into something positive. Maintain an attitude of gratitude in the restriction of affliction!

The more you practice observing from a quiet place in spirit, detaching from thoughts and emotions, and expressing gratitude in every situation, the more the soul will surrender its desire to dominate. Become the watcher!

THE WATCHER
Darrell Scott

Like sirens screaming through the streets
Like drummers pounding different beats
My thoughts are racing at a rapid pace
A joke, a story, doubt and fear
Thoughts so cloudy, thoughts so clear
They fill my mind like runners in a race

Thoughts build me up, thoughts tear me down
They jerk emotions all around
I'm drowning in a wild, chaotic sea
Some give me hope, and some despair
A lofty dream, a bad nightmare
And I have come to think that they are me

But slowly I become aware
Of Presence, sitting, waiting there
Behind the thoughts that never seem to cease
That Presence is the real me
And I have come to clearly see
That as the Watcher, I can live in peace

I'm not the thoughts I think each day
No longer guided by their sway
In stillness I can now observe their scam
The truth that's there for all to find
Is deeper than the thinking mind
The watcher is the person that I AM

Chapter 15
FINDING YOUR PURPOSE

Christians have innocently misread, misquoted and misunderstood many scriptures because that is what their parents, peers, priests, or pastors have taught them to believe. Here is an example: Matthew 7:14 KJV, says, *"Because strait is the gate, and narrow is the way, which leadeth unto life, and few there be that find it"*. There are 3 common mistakes made by well-meaning Christians who quote this verse.

Mistake #1: It is usually quoted as " the straight and narrow way". But that is not what it says. It says, *"Strait is the way, and narrow is the gate"*, not "the straight and narrow way".

Mistake #2: The word in the KJV, is *"strait"* not *"straight"*. The Greek word for *"strait"* is *"stene"* and literally means *"small"*. The Greek word for *"narrow"* is *"tethlimmene"* and literally means *"compressed"*. So the transliteration from the Greek would say, *"for small is the gate and compressed the way"*.

You will find a large variety of readings on this verse, depending on the translation you choose to read. The description directly from the Greek is that of entering into something through a small constricted entrance, similar to a baby being born.

Mistake #3: Almost all who teach on this verse, teach that the way to heaven is straight and narrow. But that is not what it is saying at all. It says that this small gate and constricted way provides the entrance into **_LIFE_** - - - not heaven!!! So the analogy of a baby being born is more accurate than that of a pilgrim on a long weary journey.

What a vast difference it makes when you compare the common explanation of this verse, versus what it really is saying. The common view is that our entire lifetime is lived through a straight and narrow pathway that eventually allows us, through death to go to heaven.

110

And few people are going to choose this "straight and narrow path", so the implication is that most people will choose the broad path to hell.

In fact, this is not describing a lifetime experience of "walking the straight and narrow" at all. It is describing a process that births us out of a purposeless existence and into a fulfilled life, here and now. And the truth is, there are few who find that entrance. Jesus came that we might have life, and life abundant.

On one occasion Jesus gave an outrageous teaching to his disciples that illustrates what we are talking about. He said, *"It is easier for a camel to go through the eye of a needle than for someone who is rich to enter the Kingdom of God"* (Matthew 19:24 NIV).

First of all he was talking about "entering the Kingdom", not "going to heaven". Big difference! You have already seen that the Kingdom of God is within you, not somewhere out in space. And you have come to understand that the Kingdom is alignment, peace, and joy. So what is this camel through the eye of a needle stuff about?

In Biblical times, cities were built with walls completely surrounding them as a defense against invaders. But, of course, there had to be gates built in to allow the citizens to travel in and out of the city. These gates were massive and thick, and would be closed and locked at night to prevent a stealth attack.

But often merchants would be traveling home from another city where they had been selling their goods, and sometimes they would return to the city with their camels (the transportation of the day) after the gates had been closed and barred to prevent an invasion.

So, the gates were designed, with a second smaller gate built into the bigger gate. It was a small enough entrance for a merchant to walk through and even bring his camels through. However, the camels had to have their saddles and all their cargo removed or they would not fit through the smaller gate.

111

In fact, the camels had to literally get down on their knees and crawl through the small gate in order to enter the city, where they would find food, shelter, and safety. Guess what this small gate was called? The eye of the needle.

So, Jesus' disciples clearly understood the analogy that he was making when he said that it was easier for a camel to go through the eye of a needle than for a rich man to enter the Kingdom. The rich man would have to "let go" of his attachment to his riches and proceed through the small gate and constricted way, in order to enter the peace and joy offered by the Kingdom. His riches could never buy him that peace and joy.

But just because he was required to let go, doesn't mean that he would have to live in poverty. The camel had to be stripped of all his or her cargo, but they didn't leave the cargo outside the gate for robbers to steal. It was brought into the city after the camel went through.

God does not require us to be poor in order to enter the Kingdom, but he does require us to "let go", to "lose our life", in order to find it. That's why in the beatitudes Jesus said, *"Blessed is the poor in spirit, for theirs is the Kingdom of Heaven"*. God's purpose is not to take away all the things that we enjoy. His purpose is to take away our attachment and dependence on the things that we enjoy.

There are a large number of Christians I have met who have a lot of "stuff", but are not living that abundant life. The abundant life is one of peace and joy, and has nothing to do with the stuff you own.

Many believe and teach that if you don't have a lot of money in the bank, own a fleet of cars and an airplane or two, and live in a mansion, then you are not living the abundant life. If that is true then Jesus and the apostles failed miserably to live the abundant life.

Paul told us the secret to abundant life when he said, *"I know what it is to be in need, and I know what it is to have plenty. I have learned the secret of being content in any and every situation, whether well*

112

fed or hungry, whether living in plenty or in want" (Philippians 4:12 NIV).

He learned that secret by finding the small, constricted entrance that led him to life. He lived abundantly in plenty and he lived abundantly in want. His soul and spirit had been separated by the Word of God. He had left his head at the altar and entered into rest! His circumstances and accumulated "stuff" had nothing to do with his identity or the abundant life that he experienced.

In this chapter I want us to look at a HUGE misinterpretation of scripture found in II Timothy 1:9. *"Who hath saved us, and called us with an holy calling, not according to our works, but according to his own purpose and grace, which was given us in Christ Jesus before the world began"*. Once again, we have a scripture that has been so misunderstood.

We are taught that God called us in order to save us. We quote scriptures, such as, *"Many are called, but few are chosen"* and we apply that to salvation. We speculate that many are called to be saved, but only a few will be.

However this verse does not say that we were called to be saved. It says that we were saved and then called. And that calling is unto a purpose - - not ours, but His! He called us, not according to our works, but to his own purpose and grace. And when was this purpose and grace given to us? It says here, *"before the world began"*.

But let's look at this verse from another translation that is much closer to what the original Greek language depicted. It is from Young's Literal Translation: *"Who did save us, and did call with an holy calling, not according to our works, but according to His own purpose and grace, that was given to us in Christ Jesus, before the times of the ages"*. Notice that the purpose and grace was given unto us before the "times of the ages".

I have heard people say, "I found God on March 17, 2015" in describing their "salvation experience". But there are 2 untruths in that statement. First of all, they didn't find God, He found them! Jesus said, *"You did not choose me, but I chose you"* (John 15:16 NIV). So, you did not chose God, he chose you. And you were not saved and called on March 17, 2015. You were saved and called to his own purpose, "before the times of the ages"!

Then He points to the purpose of why he chose us - - *"and appointed you so that you might go and bear fruit--fruit that will last--and so that whatever you ask in my name the Father will give you"*. He chose us for 3 reasons:

> #1 To go and bear fruit
> #2 To bear fruit that will last
> #3 So that whatever we ask for will be provided

Your purpose was determined millions of years before you were born. So that leads us to the most important question of all: What is my purpose? But the truth is, we need to re-align that question to say, "What is God's purpose for me? What did the Source of my being intend for me from the beginning?"

When you begin to ask, "What is your purpose for me" you are on the right track. Most people go through life trying to find their purpose in life instead of understanding what life's purpose is for them.

The prerequisite for finding purpose has been dealt with throughout this book: You must first, as Jesus said, lose your mind - - let go of your own thoughts and plans. Only then, can you enter into God's ways and thoughts.

Once you lay down your life, and enter through the small, constricted gateway that brings alignment, you will find peace, joy, purpose and abundant life. You crawled in as a caterpillar and surrendered to the cocoon, to emerge as a butterfly.

Before we can understand what "purpose" is, however, we must understand what it is not. As surprising as it may sound, your purpose is not your career, your inventions, your creations, or your accomplishments. Purpose goes much deeper than what you "do". It springs from who you are.

Most people do not know who they are. They think they are what they have or what they do. They think that they are what their ego tells them. But, as we have seen, we must "lose" that life if we are ever going to find the abundant life that Jesus spoke of.

Your number one purpose is to know the truth, proclaim the truth, and become the truth. You will then live out this purpose to everyone you meet and to everything you say and do.

"*What?*", you are probably thinking. "*What is he talking about?*" I am talking about the reason, the cause, the purpose for which Jesus came, and for the purpose for which you were born. He said it better than I could ever say it: "*for this cause came I into the world, that I should bear witness unto the truth*" (John 18:37 KJV). And you have come into this world for the same purpose.

You shall know the truth and the truth shall set you free. So, what is "the truth" that we are talking about? The truth about who you are. The Bible is full of truths about who you are, but our minds are so cluttered with our natural thoughts that we have failed to embrace these truths that are so evident. We can only become aware of who we are, and the treasure within us if we first choose to detach from the white noise of our thoughts.

If we want to bear fruit that remains, and have access to the Father with confidence that whatever we need will be supplied, then we must simply abide in the truth. Our thoughts, opinions, doctrines, tradition, and feelings are all obstacles to the truth. That's why spiritual beheading is needed.

Apply the things you have found in this book to your everyday life. You will learn to observe and detach from your thoughts, realizing

115

that they are not you. Allow the alignment to take place, even though it may be painful at times.

Allow the mountains of ecstasy to be lowered and the valleys of depression to be raised to create a straight path for the Source in your life. Stop looking for answers "out there" and realize that the treasure, the Kingdom, is within you.

Turn away from the white noise of your mind and embrace stillness and quietness in trust, for this is your strength and salvation. Abide in the truth and you will experience abundant life regardless of outward appearance or circumstances. Learn to live in the present, not the past or future. *"Behold, now is the accepted time; behold, today is the day of salvation"* (II Corinthians 6:2 KJV).

Enter into the "rest" that God has called you to by allowing the Word of God to behead you, resulting in a renewed mind. My dear friend, to paraphrase the words of Jesus: Lose your mind, and find your purpose!

CHOOSE TO LOSE
darrell scott

Lose your mind and find your purpose
Let your frenzied thinking cease
Through detachment and surrender
You will find a lasting peace

Walk the small, constricted pathway
Into life you never knew
There emerging into purpose
Realized by just a few

Lose your mind and enter stillness
Where your purpose will unfold
There your spirit will awaken
Through a quiet, resting soul

Grace and purpose will surround you
And such treasure you will find
When you yield to God's intention
And you choose to lose your mind

OTHER BOOKS BY DARRELL SCOTT

Go to Amazon and type in "books by Darrell Scott"

 Darrell Scott has authored, or co-authored 9 published books, including the best-seller, _Rachel's Tears_, the story of his daughter Rachel, the first victim of the Columbine high school shootings.

Darrell and his wife Sandy started a non-profit organization called, _Rachel's Challenge_, in Rachel's memory. Through its 40 presenters, Rachel's Challenge has reached over 28 million people in live settings over the last 18 years.

Rachel's Challenge has won 3 Emmy Awards through its television partners. They partner with Chuck and Gena Norris by providing character programming for the Norris's "KickStart Kids" organization. They also partner with the Cal Ripken, Sr. Foundation as well as with Marzano Research, one of the most prestigious K-12 research firms in the nation.

Darrell has appeared on numerous television programs such as Oprah, Larry King Live, Good Morning America, Dateline, O'Reilly Factor, Anderson Cooper, etc. He has been featured in Time magazine and quoted in Newsweek, the Wall Street Journal, and many other publications.

Darrell does keynote addresses for leadership teams of such organizations as Southwest Airlines, Bank of America, Sprint, BNSF Railroad, Motorola, and many others. He has met with Presidents Clinton, Bush, and Trump several times.

Darrell and his wife, Sandy, live in Lone Tree, Colorado where they enjoy their children and grandchildren.

Made in the USA
San Bernardino, CA
22 October 2018